The Book of Salads

The Book of Salads

An International Collection of Recipes

Sonia Uvezian

Drawings by
Wendy Wheeler

101 Productions
San Francisco

Second Printing, May, 1978
Copyright © 1977 Sonia Uvezian
Drawings copyright © 1977 Wendy Wheeler

Printed and bound in the United States of America.

Distributed to the book trade in the United States
by Charles Scribner's Sons, New York

Published by 101 Productions
834 Mission Street
San Francisco, California 94103

Library of Congress Cataloging in Publication Data

Uvezian, Sonia.
    The book of salads.

    Includes index.
    1. Salads.   I. Title.
TX740.U9   641.8'3   77-23838

ISBN 0-89286-126-6

Contents

Introduction

It is a pity that the name of the inventor of the salad has been lost in the distant past. But then I suspect that the majority of contributors to civilization, among them many individuals of greatness, have never been known to history.

Salads in one form or another have existed since time immemorial. The ancient Babylonians, Persians, Greeks, and Romans were all fond of salads and served them often. The word "salad" comes from the Latin *sal*, "salt," and is presumably derived from the early Roman custom of dipping chicory and lettuce into salt before eating them. Apicius, a Roman epicure of the first century A.D. who is said to have compiled the Western world's oldest surviving cookbook, mentions salads and lists a wide variety of vegetables and herbs. Both the Greeks and Romans served raw as well as cooked salads dressed, among other things, with oil, vinegar, and brine. The French dressing of modern times is descended from those used by the ancients.

After the fall of the Roman Empire in the West, European cuisine went into eclipse (although the civilizations of the East were not affected) and salads all but disappeared from the table. Monasteries preserved and transmitted most of what culture there was, including the art of cookery. With the coming of the Renaissance there was a marked improvement in the diet, and salads reappeared with increasing frequency. They enjoyed great popularity at the royal tables of England and France and were prepared with a remarkably wide range of ingredients.

The first book devoted to salads, *Acetaria, a Discourse of Sallets*, was written by an Englishman, John Evelyn, and appeared in 1699. However, in spite of a few notable enthusiasts, among them the French politician and gourmet Brillat-Savarin, salads suffered a setback during the eighteenth and nineteenth centuries. They have since steadily regained a position of importance on the menu, first somewhat condescendingly in our country as a favorite of the diet conscious, and later more and more because society has learned to appreciate their intrinsic wholesomeness and food value. Today salads in all their resplendent variety rank among the ultimate treats of the world's cuisines, treasured and enjoyed around the globe.

Mastering the technique of salad making is not particularly difficult, but it does require adequate planning, attention to detail, and a little practice. Even a simple tossed green salad cannot be a haphazard

7

Introduction

affair if it is to be a success. The greens must be fresh and crisp and the dressing a harmonious blend of seasonings, chosen to enhance the salad as well as the meal with which it is to be served. The proper crisping of greens and choice of ingredients for the dressing are discussed on pages 14 and 26 to 27.

A salad should not only taste good; it should look good. Visual appeal contributes greatly to one's enjoyment of any course, especially to that of the salad, which can add a refreshing touch to the menu and a splash of color to the table. The hallmark of a delectable salad, then, is a combination that offers a pleasing contrast of color as well as texture and taste.

Garnishes deserve special attention, for they can glorify even the most ordinary salad. The charm of many salads lies, at least partly, in the freshness and arrangement of their garnish. Rice, potato, pasta, and cheese salads, for instance, are not colorful in themselves. Simple garnishes such as sprigs of dark green parsley, wedges of bright red tomato, and shiny black or light green olives can make them exciting to the eye as well as the palate. However, in your efforts to present salads in an attractive form, don't go overboard. Avoid encumbering the food with elaborate garnishes, rigid aspics, and the like. Instead, play up its natural colors and textures.

The choice of bowl can also affect the appearance of a salad. Among the many different types of salad bowls available, the most popular are those made of wood, clear glass, hard grease-proof plastic, and ceramic. It is important that the bowl you use complements the particular salad as well as your table setting. It should also be suitable in color and scale with the food served. For a rustic effect, offer a tossed green salad in a wooden bowl to accompany a hearty dinner served on informal dishware and bright linen. For a more elegant occasion, you might choose a clear glass bowl and present your salad against a background of fine linen and stemmed glassware. A glass bowl makes an equally attractive container for fruit salads, or you may display a colorful array of artistically arranged fruits on a handsome platter to highlight a buffet. As an interesting change from the usual salad bowl, serve robust vegetable, pasta, or cereal salads in lettuce-lined casseroles. Many salads take on added excitement when presented in vegetable or fruit shells. Avocados, tomatoes, artichokes, oranges, melons, and pineapple all make decorative cases for salads, and lobster, crab, or clam shells lend glamor to shellfish salads. For tossing a green salad, select a wide, shallow bowl that is no deeper than three or four inches to prevent the leaves from packing or crushing. A container of generous size is always usable for lesser amounts, but a small one heaped high will overflow when tossed.

Any bowl, even a wooden one, must be washed to keep it from becoming sticky and rancid. Nowadays the surface of many fine quality wooden bowls is protected by a varnish so that it is possible to wash them in soap and warm water. They should not be allowed to soak, however. I do not recommend an untreated wooden bowl because it will absorb some of the dressing and in time become rancid. This rancidity can adversely affect the flavor of the salad.

A salad is an extremely flexible creation that lends itself to innumerable appealing combinations and serves many different purposes. It can introduce or end a meal, impart a fresh, clean taste to a hearty dinner, and function as a main course for an informal luncheon or supper. Salads play a prominent role in reducing diets, too, for salad greens and vegetables are low in calories. And if you season them imaginatively, the oil can be kept to a minimum or even be omitted entirely from the dressing.

When selecting your salad and its dressing, take into account the rest of the menu. It is important to choose an appropriate salad for a specific meal. If it is to be served as a first course or in association with the entrée, a salad must stimulate, not satiate, the appetite. It is therefore best to open a meal with a piquant salad. A main course featuring meat, fish, poultry, or a rich casserole demands a tart, leafy green salad. Vegetable, cereal, and pasta salads, most of which can be prepared in advance, are especially suitable for barbecue menus at which hearty, uncomplicated foods are served, while elaborate salads beautifully arranged and garnished, decorative mousses, and glittering aspics make ideal choices for a buffet table. Some salads are so substantial that they can be served as the main attraction of a luncheon or supper. A good choice, especially on a hot summer day, would be a meat, poultry, or seafood salad, or a chef's salad, which is really a combination salad containing, in addition to greens and vegetables, a generous amount of meat, fish, and/or cheese. The dessert salad, be it an aspic or blended fruit, provides a perfect ending to a substantial meal.

A fascinating aspect of salad making is the degree of inventiveness it encourages. By merely changing an ingredient here and there, you can give a salad an entirely new character. The recipes in this book offer a wide variety of classic as well as unusual and little-known salads and salad dressings. It is my hope that you will eventually take some liberties with these recipes and create unique dishes with the imprint of your own personality and taste.

Salad Makings

SELECTING SALAD GREENS

In today's markets, with their colorful array of tempting greens and vegetables, shopping for salad is a year-round adventure. There are a great many lettuces and other greens that can be used in salads. In addition to cultivated varieties, there are legions of wild greens that can contribute exciting flavors and textures. (Make certain, however, that you know the ones you are using and wash them very thoroughly.) Most of the greens listed below are normally obtainable in American markets. Others that may be tossed into the salad bowl include leeks, celery tops, beet tops, Swiss chard, Chinese or celery cabbage, collard greens, sea kale leaves, marigold leaves, mallow leaves, fiddleheads, and fennel. Some greens are known by different names in certain areas. These are given in parentheses.

BELGIAN ENDIVE (French Endive, Witloof). This slender, 6- to 8-inch-long, yellow-white head with tightly packed, crunchy spears has a lively, slightly bitter tang that complements blander greens in a mixed salad. It is also excellent eaten alone with a simple dressing of olive oil and lemon juice. Its distribution in America is rather limited, and when available it commands a high price indeed.

BIBB LETTUCE (Limestone). Refined and delicate, this small, cup-shaped head of soft-textured, mild green leaves is one of the finest of all lettuces.

BOSTON LETTUCE (Butter, Butterhead, Simpson). Often mistakenly called Bibb lettuce, this round, soft head, though somewhat similar to Bibb in appearance and flavor, is larger and not quite so delicate. Its tender, velvety leaves have a pleasantly mild taste, nevertheless, which will do much for a salad.

CABBAGE. A solid head having a short, thick stalk and heavy, tightly overlapping light green or reddish-purple leaves.

CHICORY (Curly Endive). This has a crown of narrow, sharply feathered leaves, shading from darkish green at the edges to a yellow-white heart. Its slightly prickly texture and rather bitter flavor goes well with blander lettuces in a tossed salad.

CORN SALAD (Lamb's Lettuce, Field Lettuce, Mâche). So called because it grows wild in cornfields, this is also cultivated commercially and in home gardens. The small, tender green leaves make a delightful salad. Widely used in France and Italy, it is not easily available in this country.

11

Salad Makings

DANDELION GREENS. Found wild in lawns, fields, meadows, and roadsides, these thin, arrowlike green leaves should be picked early in the spring while they are still young and tender. They become too tough after the flowers bloom. A cultivated variety may be found in some markets. Tart and slightly bitter, they make an interesting addition to a mixed salad.

ESCAROLE. A variety of chicory, having leaves that are broader and less curly, shading from a rich green at the edges to a pale yellow heart. Rough-textured and faintly bitter in flavor, it makes an excellent addition to a tossed salad.

ICEBERG LETTUCE (Head Lettuce). This round, firm head of tightly packed green leaves is the most familiar of American lettuces. Exceptionally crisp in texture and mild and watery in flavor, it adds a pleasant crunch to a salad.

LEAF LETTUCE (Bronze, Red, Red-Tipped Lettuce). This includes a number of varieties ranging in color from green to reddish bronze. A non-heading type that grows in large, leafy bunches, it is tender and fragile, with a sweet, delicate flavor. Good in tossed salads, it also makes an attractive undergarnish for molded salads or platter salads.

MUSTARD GREENS (Mustard Leaf, Chinese Mustard). These very curly young green leaves have a peppery, rather acrid taste. Used in salads or as a garnish. There also exists a variety known as wild mustard.

NASTURTIUM LEAVES. Peppery and somewhat like watercress in flavor, both the leaves and flowers of this decorative plant make a lovely addition to a tossed salad.

OAK LEAF LETTUCE (Australian, Salad Bowl). A variety of leaf lettuce having deeply notched leaves resembling those of an oak tree. Soft, suede-like texture; delicate in flavor.

PURSLANE (see WINTER PURSLANE).

ROCKET (Rocket Cress, Garden Rocket). Particularly well liked in Greece and also in Italy, where it is known by various names, such as *arugula*, *rugula*, and *rochetta*, this is a green with an unusual, slightly bitter, and peppery flavor. Its smooth, tender, oakleaf-shaped dark green leaves can add zest to a salad. Not easily found in American markets, it is much better known in southern Europe, where both the wild and cultivated varieties are commonly available.

ROMAINE LETTUCE (Cos). Originally exported from the Greek island of Kos. An elongated head with very crisp, spoon-shaped leaves that are dark green on the outside and pale green near the center. Succulent and slightly pungent, this is a distinctive green of superior character that combines especially well with tomato and avocado. Excellent, too, as a garnish.

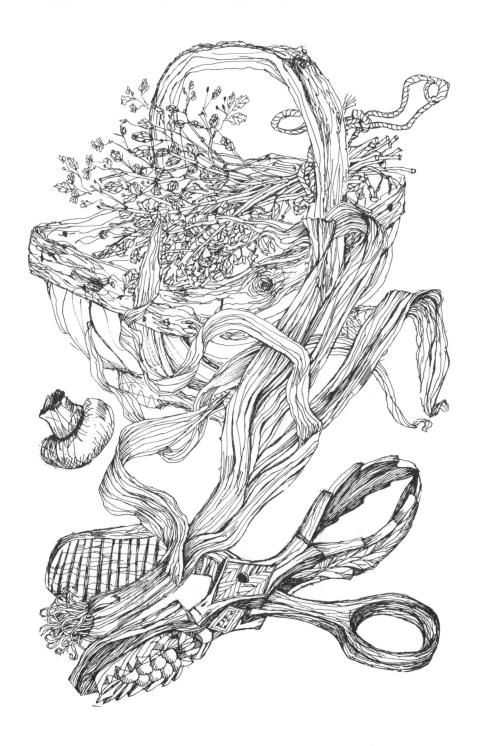

SALSIFY (Vegetable Oyster, Oyster Plant). True salsify, when found in markets, has a white-skinned root. A related plant, properly called *scorzonera*, has a black-skinned root and is more flavorful. The flesh of both is very similar in taste. The young shoots may be prepared in a variety of ways but are mainly eaten raw in salads. Wild salsify, also known as goat's beard, is found in fields and damp pastures. Its tender shoots can also be eaten in salads.

SORREL (Sour Grass). There are a number of varieties of this plant, which has been known since 3000 B.C. and which still grows wild today in many parts of the world. It is also widely cultivated. The leaves have a sour taste and are best for salads when young and tender.

SPINACH. The young, tender dark green leaves contribute an interesting flavor as well as a pleasing color contrast to other greens in a tossed salad.

WATERCRESS. This fragile plant, with long stems and glossy, dark green petal-like leaves, grows in freshwater ponds and streams. Occasionally available in markets, it has a lively, pungent flavor. A classic garnish for roasted or grilled meats, it also makes a welcome addition to a tossed green salad and a particularly attractive undergarnish for sliced tomatoes. To keep watercress, place it in a jar of water, cover, and refrigerate. A variety called winter cress, which is found wild in fields, roadsides, and streams, may be used in the same manner as watercress.

WINTER PURSLANE (Miner's Lettuce). A trailing weed with rounded, fleshy leaves. Its unusual texture and individual flavor combine well with lettuces and herbs in a mixed salad.

GUIDE TO PROPER CLEANING AND CRISPING OF SALAD GREENS

Few things detract as much from the pleasure of a good meal as a limp, soggy salad. Since at least half of the challenge, as far as a successful salad is concerned, lies in the crispness of the greens, a knowledge of how to clean, store, and prepare them is essential. Select greens that are fresh. Remove and discard any broken, wilted, or discolored leaves. Always handle greens gently, taking care not to bruise them. It is best to wash them well in advance of use in order to give them time to chill and crisp. Wash greens quickly but thoroughly under cold running water. Place them upside down in a colander to drain, then shake them gently but firmly in a French wire basket or towel to remove excess moisture. A little moisture helps crisp the leaves, while too much hastens spoilage. Wrap the greens in a damp towel or place in a clear plastic bag and store them in the vegetable crisper of your refrigerator until chilled and crisp.

When tossing time arrives, pat off any excess moisture with paper towels. The greens must be dry so that the salad dressing will cling to the leaves (wet greens dilute the dressing and make watery salads). Tear the greens into bite-size pieces. It is usual to tear rather than cut greens, although some lettuce such as iceberg or Chinese cabbage can be sliced or shredded. To help keep them crisp, toss the greens in a chilled bowl and serve on chilled plates.

THE ONION FAMILY

The members of this marvelous family deserve special attention, for many salads rely on them for their appetizing flavor. Whenever possible it is almost always preferable to use onion and garlic in their fresh state. You can, however, purchase dehydrated onion and garlic minced, powdered, and mixed with salt. Below is a list of onion types most used in salads.

BERMUDA ONIONS. Large yellow or white onions with a mild flavor.

ITALIAN ONIONS. Even milder than the Bermudas, these have a red skin and a purple-tinged flesh. Thinly sliced and separated into rings, they make a lovely garnish for salads.

SPANISH ONIONS. A good alternative to the Italian and Bermuda varieties, these are red- or yellow-skinned, mild-flavored, and flatter in shape.

SHALLOTS. These small members of the onion family, with their delicate flavor and hint of garlic, are often used in salads and salad dressings.

CHIVES. Available dried, frozen, and, when in season, fresh, this versatile plant with a refined onion flavor is used widely both as a salad ingredient and as a garnish. Good, too, in salad dressings.

SCALLIONS. Green onions. Minced scallions enhance numerous salads both as a seasoning and as a garnish. Also recommended for French and other salad dressings.

LEEKS. Believed to be a cultivated variety of Oriental garlic, leeks have a mild onionlike flavor and robust aroma. Prized for soups, they may also be used in salads.

GARLIC. A close relative of the onion, garlic possesses a strong, distinctive aroma and flavor that can lend excitement to the most ordinary salad. Use it with discretion. Crushing it with a little salt softens the bulb and helps bring out the flavor.

HERBS AND SPICES

A knowledge of herbs and spices is an essential step in becoming a fine cook, for much of the world's best cookery depends on these fragrant treasures to give it variety and excitement. Used imaginatively and discreetly, they can transform even a commonplace salad into something special.

Fresh herbs are, of course, ideal, and anyone with a patch of garden, sunny window box, or patio will find it well worth the effort to cultivate even a few varieties. Such mainstays as chives, basil, and dill are infinitely superior in their fresh state and can easily be grown. Those who are unable to obtain fresh herbs or grow their own must make do with dried ones. When substituting dried herbs for fresh, use about one-half teaspoon dried herbs for every tablespoon of chopped fresh herbs. Crush dried herbs just before using, rubbing them between your fingertips to help release their flavor and fragrance. You may freeze fresh herbs with success, chopping them beforehand if you wish. Although frozen herbs tend to be discolored and limp, they retain most of their original seasoning strength.

Since herbs and spices gradually lose their potency, buy them in small quantities, grinding or grating the latter yourself whenever possible. Store them in tightly sealed containers in a cool, dry place away from sunlight or direct heat.

The amounts given in recipes in this book for herbs and spices are approximate and may be varied to suit individual taste. However, they should not be omitted, for they play a vital role in determining the characteristic flavor of many salads.

Familiarize yourself with the flavors and aromas of the various herbs and spices and experiment, following the dictates of your own imagination and taste, always keeping in mind that the role of herbs and spices is to enhance the natural flavor of the food at hand, not to overwhelm it.

Here is a list of herbs and spices most commonly used in salads.

HERBS

BASIL. Often called sweet basil, this is one of the most versatile and savory of culinary herbs and lends a distinctive taste and fragrance to a variety of dishes. It has a classic affinity with tomatoes but also enhances seafood, eggs, greens, and vegetables such as cucumbers, green beans, kidney beans, potatoes, peas, zucchini, and eggplant. Use it in rice or pasta salads and in French dressing. Basil can easily be grown in a sunny location.

BAY LEAF. An important ingredient in marinades, court bouillons, stocks, and sauces, this strongly aromatic herb is frequently used to flavor seafood and vegetable aspics. Use it with discretion.

BURNET. Also known as salad burnet, this herb has a taste reminiscent of cucumbers. Use in green and vegetable salads.

CAPERS. Used extensively as a condiment as well as a garnish, capers add a piquancy to many salads and are especially compatible with fish, poultry, and tomatoes.

CHIVES. See page 15.

CHERVIL. A great favorite in French cookery, where it is used in the classic *fines herbes* combination, as a garnish, and in salad dressings and salads, including green, vegetable, egg, chicken, and, particularly, potato salad. Try to use fresh chervil whenever possible, for the leaves lose much of their taste when dried.

CORIANDER LEAVES (Chinese Parsley, Cilantro). An herb resembling flat-leaf parsley but having a much stronger flavor. The green leaves, which have a distinctive odor, taste entirely different from the seeds. Fresh coriander is widely used both in food preparation and as a garnish in Latin American, Indian, Caucasian, Middle Eastern, Oriental, and Portuguese cooking. In the United States it can be found in Latin American and Chinese markets. You can grow your own coriander by planting the seeds. If, however, you dislike the smell and taste of this herb, you can omit it entirely or substitute flat-leaf parsley.

DILL. When in season, fresh dill is often available in the market. The dried leaves and seeds may be purchased in jars. Both the seeds and feathery leaves of this moderately aromatic herb harmonize perfectly with sour cream, cabbage, cucumber, green beans, potato salad, and seafood.

FENNEL (Finocchio). This has a pleasant anise-like flavor. Both the fleshy bulbous stem and the leaves of fennel are used frequently in Italian and French cooking. The stem, for which the Italians have a particular fondness, can be eaten raw or cooked. It is often shredded and added to salads.

GARLIC. See page 15.

MARJORAM (Sweet Marjoram). A versatile and very popular herb, marjoram can be used in French dressing as well as in poultry, egg, seafood, and vegetable salads incorporating spinach, peas, lima beans, or green beans.

MINT. This refreshing herb, with a penetrating aroma and lively taste, makes a delightful contribution to French dressing and salads made with fruits, greens, and vegetables such as tomatoes, cucumbers, cabbage, zucchini, eggplant, peas, lima beans, and beets. There exist numerous varieties of mint, each one differing considerably in flavor and fragrance. When in season, fresh mint is occasionally found in some markets. You can easily grow your own mint at home.

OREGANO (Wild Marjoram). Lustier and more assertive than sweet marjoram, this fragrantly potent herb is used extensively in Greek, Italian, and Latin American kitchens. A classic seasoning for tomatoes, it also imparts pungency to green, artichoke, eggplant, potato, kidney bean, pasta, egg, cheese, meat, and seafood salads. Good, too, in French dressing.

PARSLEY. A universally popular and most useful herb, parsley is valuable both as a flavoring agent and as a garnish. There are two principal varieties: curly parsley, the type most commonly seen in markets; and flat-leaf or Italian parsley. Rich in vitamins and minerals, parsley is used in many green, vegetable, egg, cereal, pasta, seafood, poultry, and meat salads. It keeps well in the refrigerator in a jar of water.

ROSEMARY. When used sparingly, this strongly aromatic herb makes a pleasing addition to seafood, chicken, turkey, and lamb salads.

SAVORY. A classic seasoning for bean salads, this delicately flavored herb is also good with peas and tomatoes, in vegetable salads, and in French dressing.

18

TARRAGON. This popular herb, with a rather sophisticated flavor hinting of anise, is often added to green salads in France, alone or in combination with chervil and chives. Used discreetly, it also imparts a subtle flavor and fragrance to tomato, seafood, chicken, and fruit salads as well as some salad dressings, including mayonnaise. Tarragon vinegar, incidentally, is ordinary vinegar in which small tarragon shoots have been steeped.

THYME. Used judiciously, this moderately pungent herb adds a pleasant touch to egg, chicken, meat, tomato, and most vegetable salads.

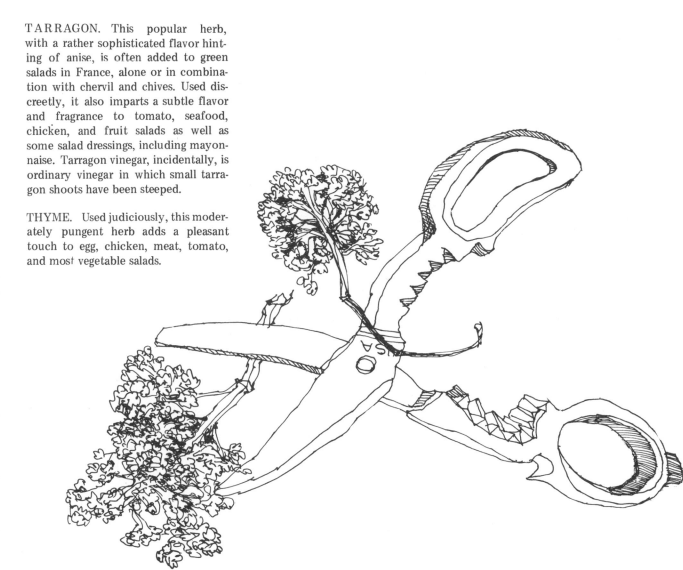

SPICES

ALLSPICE. Within the berry of this tropical tree lies the combined flavor and fragrance of cinnamon, nutmeg, and cloves, hence its name. Used both whole and ground in fruit salads.

CARAWAY SEEDS. A classic addition to rye bread, these seeds impart a tangy aroma to cheese, potato, and cabbage salads as well. Crush them before using to release their full flavor and fragrance.

CARDAMOM SEEDS. These aromatic seeds are available whole or ground. Used frequently in pickling spice mixtures, they are also recommended for fruit salads and compotes.

CAYENNE (Cayenne Pepper). A powder made from very hot varieties of capsicum red peppers, cayenne is one of the most pungent of spices. Use it very sparingly to add a fiery bite to salad dressings.

CELERY SALT. Commonly found in pickling spice mixtures, this blend of ground celery seeds and ordinary table salt may also be used in salads and salad dressings.

CHILI POWDER. This is usually composed of chili pepper, oregano, cumin, and garlic. However, depending on the manufacturer, other spices such as ground cloves, allspice, coriander, and black pepper may also be included. A popular seasoning for Mexican-style dishes, chili powder lends an invigorating taste to vegetable, egg, and seafood salads as well as salad dressings.

CINNAMON. A warm, sweet, aromatic spice that boasts a universal appeal. Available whole or ground, it is used to flavor and perfume all manner of dishes including fruit salads.

CLOVES. These nail-shaped buds, which may be purchased whole or ground, are among the most pungent of spices. Used in fruit salads.

CORIANDER SEEDS. Available whole or ground, these pleasantly aromatic seeds are used in salad dressings, pickling mixtures, and marinades.

CUMIN SEEDS. Originally from Egypt, where they were used with meats and fish. Today cumin continues to be an important seasoning in Middle Eastern cookery, including salads. It is also a popular ingredient in Latin American salads.

CURRY POWDER. A combination of ground spices that lends an exotic character to seafood, poultry, egg, potato, tomato, rice, and fruit salads and to mayonnaise and French dressing.

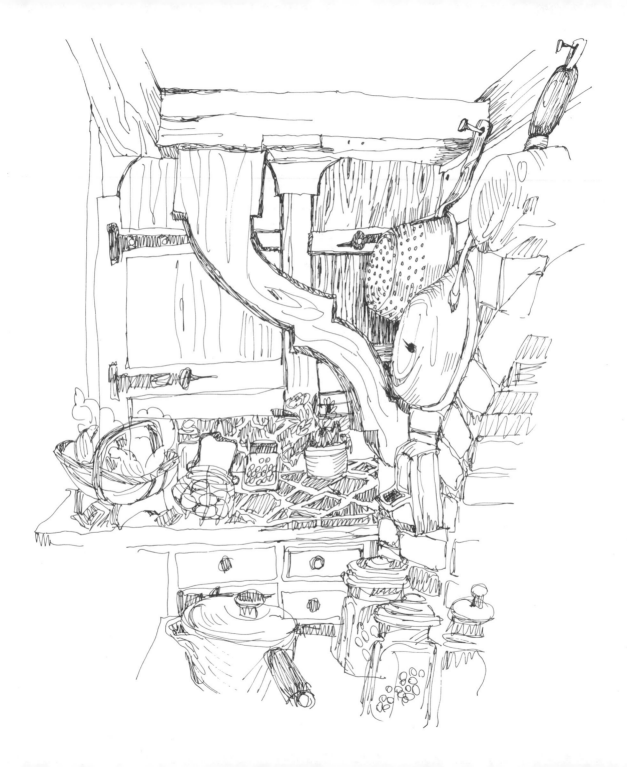

GINGER. Available whole or ground, this has a spicy-sweet, pungent flavor that adds interest to fruit salads.

MUSTARD. A hot, sharp spice that comes in three forms: whole seeds, ground, and prepared mustard, which is one of the most popular condiments in America. Mustard seeds, which range in color from white to yellow to dark brown, are added to relishes, pickles, and cole slaw. Ground and prepared mustard may be used in most salad dressings.

NUTMEG. Although this may be purchased already ground, it is superior in flavor when freshly grated. Use it sparingly to lend a sweet, warm, and spicy taste to fruit salads.

PAPRIKA. Valuable both as a garnish and as a seasoning, this brilliantly red powder, ground from sweet red peppers, enlivens salads and dressings.

PEPPER. Pepper berries intended for sale as black pepper are picked just before they are completely ripe, while those to be marketed as white pepper are allowed to ripen fully. This simplifies the removal of the dark outer shell, leaving only the inner, light-colored kernel. Both peppers are available as peppercorns as well as in fine and coarse grind. There is some difference in flavor, black pepper being somewhat stronger than white, but their use is practically interchangeable. White pepper is preferred for light-colored foods where specks of black pepper would be unattractive, as in white sauces, some mayonnaises, and fruit salads. The difference in flavor and aroma between freshly ground and pre-ground pepper is enormous. It is therefore always preferable to buy whole peppercorns and grind them in a peppermill as required. Pepper is a stimulant that plays an important role in many culinary preparations, including most salad dressings.

POPPY SEEDS. Usually colored a slate blue (though there also exists a white variety), these tiny seeds lend a crunchy texture and nutlike flavor to salad greens, cole slaw, and fruit salads. Toasting them before using enhances their taste.

RED PEPPER. Slightly less fiery than cayenne, this spice is available whole, crushed, and ground. Whole red peppers are used in relishes and pickles. Crushed red peppers, sometimes called "pizza peppers," are a vital ingredient in many Italian and Latin American dishes, including salads. Ground red pepper may be added to salad dressings. Use it with caution.

SESAME SEEDS. Known since ancient times, these provide a delightful texture when added to salad dressings or sprinkled on green, vegetable, fruit, and chicken salads. Their delicate, nutty flavor is heightened when the seeds are lightly toasted. Sesame seed paste *(tahini)* and sesame oil, both used in salad dressings, are derived from sesame seeds.

TURMERIC. An important ingredient in pickling and relish making, this rather bitter, orange-yellow spice also gives flavor and color to prepared mustard as well as egg, potato, and chicken salads. Use it with discretion.

Salad Makings

APPROPRIATE HERBS
AND SPICES FOR SALADS

Below is a list of ingredients frequently used in salads and suggestions for compatible herbs and spices.

ARTICHOKES. Basil, oregano, curry powder.

BEANS. Basil, coriander, dill, mint, oregano, parsley, savory, tarragon, thyme, cayenne.

BEETS. Bay leaf, chervil, dill, mint, parsley, tarragon, thyme, cloves, toasted sesame seeds.

CABBAGE. Basil, dill, mint, anise, caraway seeds, poppy seeds.

CAULIFLOWER. Basil, dill, marjoram, paprika, toasted sesame seeds.

CHEESE. Basil, oregano, caraway seeds, cayenne, chili powder, mustard, paprika.

CUCUMBERS. Basil, dill, mint, tarragon, cayenne, chili powder.

EGGS. Chervil, dill, marjoram, oregano, parsley, tarragon, cayenne, chili powder, cumin, curry powder, mustard, paprika.

EGGPLANT. Basil, coriander, dill, mint, oregano, toasted sesame seeds.

FISH AND SHELLFISH. Basil, capers, dill, mint, oregano, parsley, tarragon, thyme, cayenne, chili powder, cumin, curry powder.

FRUIT. Mint, rosemary, tarragon, allspice, cardamom, cayenne, cinnamon, chili powder, cloves, coriander, ginger, nutmeg, paprika, toasted sesame seeds.

GREENS. Basil, chervil, dill, marjoram, mint, oregano, parsley, tarragon, thyme.

MEAT. Basil, chervil, dill, oregano, parsley, rosemary, tarragon, thyme, cayenne, cumin, curry powder.

PASTA. Basil, oregano, parsley, cayenne.

POTATOES. Basil, dill, oregano, parsley, savory, caraway seeds, celery seeds, chili powder, curry powder, paprika.

POULTRY. Basil, capers, chervil, fennel, marjoram, parsley, rosemary, tarragon, thyme, cumin, curry powder, toasted sesame seeds.

RICE. Basil, parsley, curry powder.

TOMATOES. Basil, chervil, dill, marjoram, mint, oregano, parsley, savory, tarragon, thyme, cumin.

Salad Makings

OILS AND VINEGARS

The importance of using excellent quality oil and vinegar cannot be overstressed. My own preference is for olive oil in almost all dressings, and anyone with a taste for natural food will appreciate the flavor of good olive oil, which, incidentally, is an easily digested, monounsaturated type of fat that neither raises nor lowers the cholesterol level in the blood.

Although there are three different grades of olive oil, only two are suitable for cooking. The best grade is extracted from finest-quality olives that have been crushed, without any application of heat. It has a distinctive, clean, and fruity flavor and keeps well. A less desirable grade of olive oil is extracted by pressure under heat. It is light in body and color and tends to become rancid more rapidly when exposed to the air. People unaccustomed to the natural taste of olive oil may prefer the blander light-bodied, light-colored type.

A number of countries, among them Greece, Italy, France, and Spain, produce olive oil. Try various kinds to find your favorite. The flavors of olive oils are affected by the different soils in which olive trees grow. Connoisseurs choose their oil as carefully as some people choose their wine. Oils from the regions of Provence in southern France, Liguria and Lucca in Italy, and the Italian island of Sardina are held in particularly high esteem.

Other oils that may be used in salad dressings include those made from corn, cottonseeds, peanuts, poppyseeds, safflower seeds, soybeans, and sunflower seeds. Although less expensive than olive oil, these are almost tasteless and lack the former's delicate aroma. If, however, you find the taste of olive oil too strong (or the price too high!), you might try combining it with one of these blander oils. Polyunsaturated oils such as corn, cottonseed, safflower, soybean, or sunflower would be good choices for the cholesterol conscious. When recipes in this book call for vegetable oil, any of the above may be used. Two other oils that are occasionally employed in dressings are sesame oil and walnut oil. Both have a pronounced nutty flavor that, as might be expected, limits their use. The sesame oil called for in the recipes in this book is Oriental sesame oil, which should not be confused with the mild sesame oil found in some markets.

Vinegars vary greatly and make a tremendous difference in the final outcome of a dressing. Personally, I prefer to use a red or white wine vinegar that is not overly strong in the vast majority of recipes calling for vinegar. In Europe wine vinegar is generally favored; in America, however, cider vinegar continues to be popular. Unless specified, either red or white wine vinegar may be used in recipes calling for wine vinegar.

A good wine vinegar is clear, has a definite acid taste, and an aroma recalling that of the wine from which it is derived. The finest French wine vinegars come from Orléans. Others of good quality include some Italian and domestic brands.

Vinegars flavored with herbs, spices, garlic, shallots, raspberries, rose petals, and elder flowers (to mention only some) can add interest to a dressing. You can easily transform a good cider or wine vinegar into herbed vinegar. Traditional vinegar herbs for the table include basil, burnet, chervil, marjoram, mint, oregano, rosemary, savory, tarragon, and thyme. To make herbed vinegar, choose an individual herb or a combination of herbs, using three tablespoons fresh herb leaves per quart of cider or wine vinegar. (One

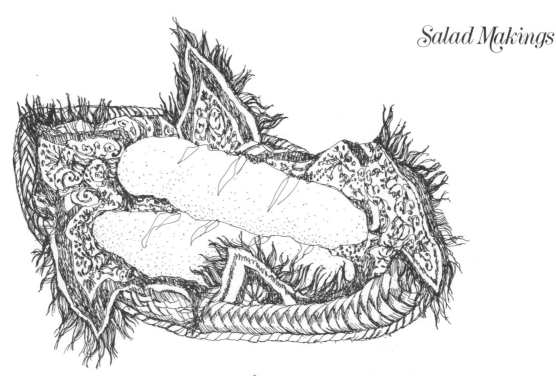

clove garlic, crushed, may also be added, but remove it after 24 hours.) Allow to steep four weeks. Strain the vinegar through a funnel lined with a cloth into sterilized bottles and keep tightly corked.

When using lemon (or lime) juice rather than vinegar, be sure it is freshly squeezed and strained. If allowed to stand many hours, it tends to acquire a rancid taste that can noticeably affect the flavor of a dressing.

In dressings of the French (vinaigrette) type, the proportion of oil to vinegar (or lemon juice) can vary according to personal taste. The ratio usually ranges from one part oil and one part vinegar to four parts oil and one part vinegar.

HOW TO MAKE CROÛTONS

Use as many slices of day-old white bread (preferably French bread or other firm-textured breads such as whole wheat, rye, or pumpernickel) as desired. Trim the crusts off or not as you wish. Cut each slice into 1/2-inch cubes. In a heavy skillet heat a small amount of butter or oil (preferably olive oil) over moderate heat (1 cup bread cubes will require about 1 tablespoon butter or oil). Add the bread cubes and sauté until golden brown and crisp all over, stirring frequently. Alternately, toss the bread cubes in melted butter or oil (or brush the bread slices with butter, then cube them) and place them on an ungreased baking sheet. Bake in a preheated 400° oven about 10 to 12 minutes or until golden brown and crisp, turning so they color evenly on all sides.

Seasoned Croûtons When the bread cubes are almost done, sprinkle them to taste with curry powder, chili powder, garlic salt, crushed dried thyme or marjoram, or other desired seasoning.

Garlic Croûtons Sauté 1 clove garlic, crushed, in the heated butter until golden brown. Remove and discard. Add the bread cubes and proceed as directed above.

Cheese Croûtons When the bread cubes are almost done, sprinkle them with freshly grated Swiss or Parmesan cheese. Continue to sauté or bake them just until the cheese melts.

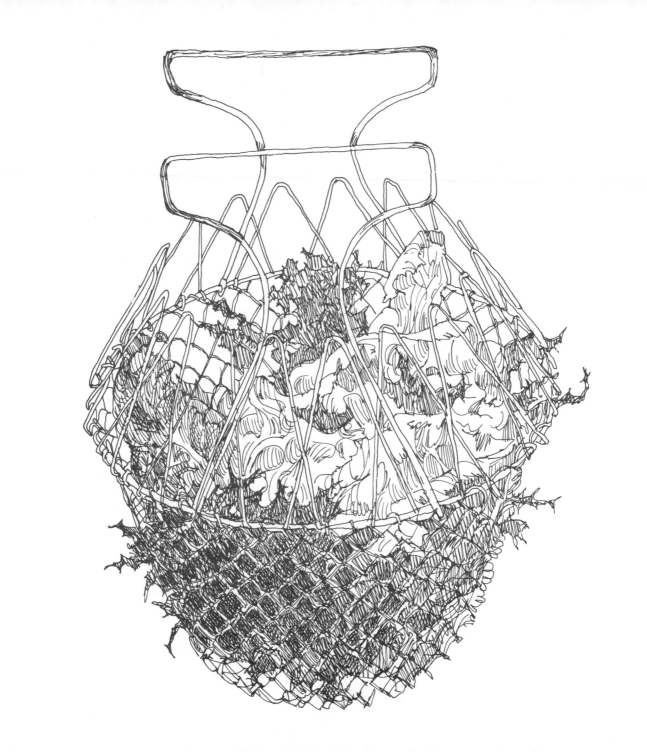

Green Salads

A green salad is the most popular and versatile of all salads. It stimulates the appetite, complements a rich entrée, and furnishes essential vitamins and minerals. When properly made, it can be a great asset to a meal.

Basically, a green salad is composed only of greens and a suitable dressing. If other ingredients are included, don't be too lavish with them. Their role should be to enhance, not dominate.

A marvelous selection of salad greens is available in American markets. Some of the most widely used are listed on pages 11 through 14. A tossed green salad is delicious made with crisp succulent romaine, soft buttery Boston lettuce, tender ruffled leaf lettuce, crunchy sweet iceberg, curly fringed chicory, or peppery dark green watercress, to mention only a few. To achieve interesting contrast in flavor and texture as well as color, combine several different greens.

Chopped fresh herbs are a splendid addition to a green salad. So are certain fruits and vegetables such as orange or grapefruit sections, avocado, tomato, cucumber, green pepper, thinly sliced onion or scallions, raw or cooked mushrooms, and cooked artichoke hearts. Other possibilities include green or black olives; grated or crumbled cheese; toasted sesame seeds, almonds, filberts, or walnuts; croûtons; crumbled crisp bacon; and anchovies.

The position of a green salad on the menu is a matter of ever-changing custom. At one time the Romans served lettuce at the conclusion of the evening meal, as the Persians still do. Near the end of the first century, however, during the reign of the emperor Domitian, it became the fashion to offer lettuce as an appetizer. Nowadays it is a matter of personal choice whether to have a tossed green salad before, during, or after the main course. Most Americans like to serve it as an accompaniment to the entrée, although in California (and in many restaurants) it is usually presented as the first course. Europeans, on the other hand, tend to serve salad before or after the main course in order to prevent the salad vinegar from interfering with the wines of the meal. If served after the main course, it can be accompanied with or followed by cheese and crackers.

Green Salads

HOW TO DRESS
A GREEN SALAD

There are two basic methods of adding the dressing to a green salad. In the first, it is mixed in advance in a jar or in the bottom of the empty salad bowl and tossed with the greens just before serving in order to prevent them from becoming soggy. When tossed, each leaf should be well coated with the dressing but not dripping with it, and there should not be an accumulation of dressing in the bottom of the bowl.

In the second, more classic, method the dressing ingredients are added directly to the greens one at a time, beginning with the oil, followed by the seasonings, and ending with the vinegar (or fresh lemon juice).

If you wish to make a ceremony of the tossing of your salad, have the oil, vinegar, and seasonings ready at the table when you bring in the bowl of chilled torn salad greens. Sprinkle measured tablespoons of oil over the greens (use 4 to 6 tablespoons oil for every 3 quarts greens), and toss repeatedly by lifting the leaves gently with a large salad fork and spoon until each leaf is thoroughly coated. The oil not only prevents the vinegar from wilting the greens when it is poured over them but helps other seasonings to adhere to the leaves as well. Next, sprinkle with salt and freshly ground pepper to taste (or any other seasonings you plan to add to your salad, such as fresh or dried herbs, minced scallions, crumbled crisp bacon, etc.). Finally, sprinkle measured tablespoons of vinegar over the salad (use 2 to 3 tablespoons for every 4 to 6 tablespoons oil), toss again, and serve at once. Mixed according to this technique, your salad will stay crisp and appetizing.

If you want to toss the salad at table without the production of measuring and mixing the ingredients for the dressing, you can prepare the dressing ahead in the bottom of the empty salad bowl, cross the salad fork and spoon over it, pile the greens on top, and refrigerate. When serving time arrives, bring the bowl to the table and toss the salad.

When tossing a bowl of salad greens, hold cut-up tomatoes till last in order to prevent diluting the dressing. Or dress them separately and use them for garnishing the salad bowl.

A word about garlic: There are several ways of adding it to a salad. One way is to rub the inside of the salad bowl with a split clove of garlic before adding the greens and the dressing. Another is to rub a dry crust of bread or *chapon*, as it is called in the southwest of France, on all sides with a cut clove of garlic. Combine the bread in the bowl with the salad greens, add the dressing, and toss the salad. Remove the bread before serving the salad. For a stronger garlic flavor, crush a clove of garlic at the bottom of the salad bowl with a little salt before adding the oil and vinegar. This softens the bulb and releases the flavor, allowing it to mingle deliciously with the salad greens when tossed.

TOSSED GREEN SALAD

The charm of this basic salad lies in its simplicity.

Serves 6

3 quarts torn assorted salad greens
   (romaine, chicory, escarole, or
   other salad greens)
1 tablespoon finely chopped chives
   or scallions (include 2 inches of
   the green tops of the scallions)
1 tablespoon finely chopped parsley
1 tablespoon finely chopped basil or
   tarragon (optional)
1/2 cup French Dressing, page 138

Combine the salad greens, chives, parsley, and basil in a salad bowl. Add the dressing and toss gently but thoroughly.

Variation Sprinkle 2 tablespoons freshly grated Parmesan cheese over the salad just before serving. A delicious, though not classic, addition.

SALADE MIMOSA

Hard-cooked eggs and fresh herbs lend a distinctive touch to this favorite French salad.

Serves 4

1 medium head Boston lettuce, torn
   into bite-size pieces
1 hard-cooked egg
2 tablespoons finely chopped parsley,
   tarragon, and/or basil
Salt and freshly ground black pepper
   to taste
1/3 cup Garlic French Dressing,
   page 138

Place the lettuce in a salad bowl. Force the egg through a fine wire strainer and mix with the parsley and salt and pepper. Pour the dressing over the lettuce and toss gently but thoroughly. Sprinkle with the egg mixture and serve immediately.

GREEN SALAD WITH TOMATO AND AVOCADO

The soft, buttery texture and taste of the avocado provides a pleasing contrast to the crunchiness of the lettuce and sweet acidity of the tomatoes.

Serves 6

3 medium tomatoes, peeled, seeded,
   and cut into wedges
1 large avocado, peeled, pitted, and
   sliced
2 scallions, finely chopped, including
   2 inches of the green tops
1/2 cup French Dressing, page 138
1 small head romaine lettuce, torn
   into bite-size pieces
3 tablespoons freshly grated Parmesan
   or Romano cheese

Combine the tomatoes, avocado, scallions, and dressing in a salad bowl. Cover and refrigerate 30 minutes, stirring 2 or 3 times. Just before serving, add the lettuce and cheese and toss gently but thoroughly. Taste and adjust the seasoning.

GREEN SALAD WITH CROÛTONS

Croûtons impart flavor as well as an interesting texture to this herb-scented combination shaded with garlic.

Serves 4

6 cups torn salad greens (romaine, Boston, and chicory)
1/4 cup finely chopped chives or scallions (include 2 inches of the green tops of the scallions)
1 small red onion, peeled, cut crosswise into 1/8-inch-thick slices, and separated into rings
1/4 cup pitted black olives
1/2 cup croûtons, page 27
1/4 cup olive oil
1 tablespoon freshly squeezed and strained lemon juice
1 tablespoon red wine vinegar
1 tiny clove garlic, crushed
1/2 teaspoon crushed dried tarragon
1/2 teaspoon crushed dried basil
1 teaspoon salt
1/4 teaspoon freshly ground black pepper

Place the salad greens, chives, onion, olives, and croûtons in a salad bowl. Beat together the remaining ingredients with a fork or whisk until well blended and pour over the salad. Toss gently but thoroughly; serve at once.

CAESAR SALAD

A California specialty that has achieved nationwide recognition.

Serves 8

1 medium clove garlic
3/4 cup olive oil
2 cups white bread cubes (preferably made from stale French bread)
2 heads romaine lettuce, torn into bite-size pieces
1/2 teaspoon salt
1/4 teaspoon freshly ground black pepper
2 eggs
1/4 cup freshly squeezed and strained lemon juice or to taste
8 anchovy fillets, finely chopped
1/2 cup freshly grated Parmesan cheese

Crush the garlic in a small bowl. Add the oil and let stand 1 hour. In a heavy skillet heat 1/4 cup of the garlic oil over moderate heat. Add the bread cubes and fry until golden brown on all sides. Remove from the heat and set aside.

Place the lettuce in a salad bowl. Sprinkle with the salt and pepper. Pour over the remaining 1/2 cup garlic oil and toss gently but thoroughly to coat each lettuce leaf with it. Use the eggs raw, or cook them 1 minute in gently boiling water. Break the eggs into the salad and toss thoroughly. Add the lemon juice and anchovies and toss again. Add the fried bread cubes and cheese. Toss a final time and serve at once.

Variations Wine vinegar or a mixture of wine vinegar and lemon juice may be substituted for the lemon juice. One-fourth cup each freshly grated Parmesan cheese and crumbled Roquefort cheese may be used rather than Parmesan alone.

Green Salads

CHEF'S SALAD

Chef's salad, an American invention, consists of a bowlful of greens and vegetables and some form of protein, such as meat, chicken, fish, or cheese, arranged for maximum eye appeal. It should be tossed at the table, after the diners have seen the arrangement of the salad. Instead of using one large bowl, you may arrange the salad in individual chef-size salad bowls for each person, in which case you might offer a choice of dressings.

34

Serves 6

1 head romaine lettuce, torn into
    bite-size pieces
1 head Boston lettuce, torn into
    bite-size pieces
Several leaves each escarole, chicory,
    and iceberg lettuce, torn into
    bite-size pieces
1 bunch watercress, trimmed
1 medium cucumber, peeled and
    sliced
3 scallions, finely chopped, including
    2 inches of the green tops
2 cups julienne-cut cooked ham
2 cups julienne-cut Italian salami
12 ounces Swiss cheese, cut in
    julienne
3 hard-cooked eggs, quartered
12 small cherry tomatoes, or
    2 tomatoes, cut into wedges
12 pitted black olives
3/4 cup Italian Dressing, page 143

Combine the lettuce, watercress, cucumber, and scallions in a large, shallow salad bowl. Toss together, making a bed. Arrange alternating bundles of ham, salami, and cheese strips in a decorative pattern on top of the lettuce. Garnish with the eggs, tomatoes, and olives. Pour the dressing over all and toss at table.

LOBSTER CHEF'S SALAD

Serves 4

4 cups torn salad greens (romaine,
    Boston, chicory or escarole, and
    watercress or spinach)
1 medium avocado, peeled, pitted,
    and cubed
2 medium tomatoes, peeled, seeded,
    and cubed
4 scallions, thinly sliced, including
    2 inches of the green tops
1 grapefruit, peeled, seeded, and
    sectioned (remove the white
    membrane)
8 ounces diced cooked lobster meat
8 pitted black olives, sliced
1/2 cup Lemon French Dressing,
    page 138

Place the greens in a salad bowl and toss them together. Arrange all the remaining ingredients except the dressing in an attractive pattern over the greens. Pour the dressing over and toss at table.

NEW ORLEANS CHEF'S SALAD

Serves 4

4 cups torn salad greens (Boston,
    chicory, and watercress or spinach)
1 stalk celery, thinly sliced
4 scallions, thinly sliced, including
    2 inches of the green tops
2 medium tomatoes, peeled and
    quartered
1 medium avocado, peeled, pitted, and
    thinly sliced
2 hard-cooked eggs, quartered
8 ounces cooked crab meat
8 ounces cooked small shrimp
1/4 cup pitted black olives
2 tablespoons chopped parsley
1/2 cup Lemon French Dressing,
    page 138

Place the greens in a salad bowl and toss them together. Arrange all the remaining ingredients except the dressing in a decorative pattern on top of the greens. Pour the dressing over and toss at table.

Green Salads

GREEK TOSSED SALAD

Salads are popular throughout Greece, and none more so than the one described below.

Serves 4

4 cups torn salad greens (romaine, chicory, and escarole)
1 large tomato, seeded and cut into wedges
1 small green pepper, seeded, deribbed, and cut into thin rings
1 small red or Bermuda onion, cut crosswise into 1/8-inch-thick slices and separated into rings
1 medium cucumber, peeled and sliced (optional)
6 radishes, thinly sliced
8 black olives (preferably imported Calamata or Alonso olives)
4 anchovy fillets
6 tablespoons olive oil
2 tablespoons freshly squeezed and strained lemon juice or wine vinegar
Salt and freshly ground black pepper to taste
1 teaspoon crushed dried oregano
1/4 cup crumbled feta cheese

Combine the salad greens, tomato, green pepper, onion, cucumber, radishes, olives, and anchovies in a salad bowl. Beat together the oil, lemon juice, salt and pepper, and oregano with a fork or whisk until well blended and pour over the salad. Toss gently but thoroughly. Sprinkle with the cheese and serve immediately.

Note When in season, 2 tablespoons minced mint may be substituted for the oregano.

MEXICAN SALAD

The Mexicans have devised some exciting and original salads to contribute to the world's cuisine. The following lively spiced combination is a flavorful accompaniment to beef or chicken.

Serves 6

2 tablespoons butter
1 medium clove garlic, minced
6 slices French bread, cut into 1/2-inch cubes
1 medium head iceberg lettuce, torn into bite-size pieces
1 cup diced cooked and peeled potato
1/2 cup thinly sliced celery
1/2 cup finely sliced mild onion, separated into rings
1/2 green pepper, seeded, deribbed, and thinly sliced
6 tablespoons olive oil or vegetable oil
3 tablespoons white wine vinegar
3/4 teaspoon chili powder
1/4 teaspoon crushed dried oregano
1/2 teaspoon superfine sugar
Salt and freshly ground black pepper to taste
1 medium avocado, peeled, pitted, and sliced
Juice of 1 lime, freshly squeezed and strained
1/3 cup pimiento-stuffed olives, cut in half crosswise

In a heavy skillet heat the butter and garlic over moderate heat. Add the bread cubes and fry until golden brown on all sides. Remove from the heat and drain on absorbent paper. In a salad bowl combine the lettuce, potato, celery, onion, green pepper, and fried bread cubes. Mix together the oil, vinegar, chili powder, oregano, sugar, and salt and pepper and pour over the salad. Toss gently but thoroughly. Taste and adjust the seasoning. Decorate the top with the avocado slices, which have been sprinkled with the lime juice, and the olives. Serve immediately.

37

ARMENIAN SPINACH SALAD

If you have any prejudice against spinach, do try to suspend it long enough to sample this exceptional dish.

Serves 4

2 bunches spinach
2 medium cucumbers, peeled, quartered lengthwise (cut out the seeds if too large and discard), and thinly sliced
1/3 cup pitted black olives, sliced
1/3 cup pitted green olives, sliced (optional)
1/4 cup thinly sliced red or Bermuda onion
1/2 cup finely chopped parsley
2 tablespoons chopped salted and roasted pistachios or pine nuts
1/4 cup olive oil
2 tablespoons freshly squeezed and strained lemon juice or wine vinegar
Salt and freshly ground black pepper to taste
Pinch crushed dried oregano

38

Wash the spinach thoroughly under cold running water. Remove the stems. Dry the spinach leaves and break them into bite-size pieces. Combine the spinach, cucumbers, olives, onion, parsley, and pistachios in a salad bowl. Beat the remaining ingredients with a fork or whisk until blended and pour over the salad. Toss gently but thoroughly and serve immediately.

SPINACH AND BACON SALAD

Serves 6
2 pounds spinach
1 large avocado, peeled, pitted, and diced
8 slices bacon, cooked crisp and crumbled
3 hard-cooked eggs, chopped
1/2 cup French Dressing, page 138
1/2 cup chopped roasted peanuts

Wash the spinach thoroughly under cold running water. Remove the stems. Dry the spinach leaves and break into bite-size pieces. Combine the spinach, avocado, bacon, and eggs in a salad bowl. Add the dressing and toss gently but thoroughly. Sprinkle with the peanuts and serve at once.

Variation Add 4 scallions, thinly sliced, with the avocado and omit the peanuts.

WILTED LETTUCE

Serves 4
1 quart torn leaf lettuce
2 tablespoons finely chopped mild onion or scallions (include 2 inches of the green tops)
2 hard-cooked eggs, coarsely chopped (optional)
3 slices bacon, cut into 1/2-inch pieces
3 tablespoons mild vinegar or freshly squeezed and strained lemon juice
1 teaspoon sugar
1/4 teaspoon dry mustard
Salt and freshly ground black pepper to taste

Combine the lettuce, onion, and eggs in a large salad bowl and set aside. In a small, heavy skillet cook the bacon over moderate heat until crisp, turning frequently. Add the vinegar, sugar, mustard, and salt and pepper to the bacon and drippings and heat, stirring, until the sugar dissolves. Pour the mixture over the ingredients in the salad bowl and toss gently but thoroughly. Taste and adjust the seasoning. Serve immediately.

Variation Dandelion leaves or a mixture of leaf lettuce, dandelion leaves, spinach, or other greens may be substituted for the leaf lettuce.

Wilted Lettuce with Tomato Variation Substitute 1 large tomato, peeled, seeded, and chopped, for the eggs and 1/2 teaspoon crushed dried oregano or mint for the mustard.

HEARTS OF PALM AND AVOCADO SALAD

Serves 6
1/2 head romaine lettuce, torn into bite-size pieces
1/2 head escarole, torn into bite-size pieces
1 16-ounce can hearts of palm, drained and cut crosswise into thin slices
2 avocados, peeled, pitted, and sliced
3 scallions, thinly sliced, including 2 inches of the green tops
1/4 cup pimiento-stuffed olives
Pimiento strips
Hard-cooked egg slices (optional)
1/2 cup Garlic French Dressing, page 138
1/4 teaspoon crushed dried tarragon

Place the greens in a salad bowl and toss together. Arrange all the remaining ingredients except the dressing and tarragon in a decorative pattern over the greens. Combine the dressing and tarragon and pour over the salad. Toss at table.

Green Salads

ENDIVE AND APPLE SALAD WITH WALNUTS

Serves 4

4 heads Belgian endive, cut into
    bite-size pieces
2 medium apples, peeled, cored,
    and cut into bite-size pieces
1/3 cup walnut meats, coarsely
    chopped (preferably freshly
    shelled)
1/4 cup olive oil
2 tablespoons freshly squeezed and
    strained lemon juice
Salt to taste

Combine the endive, apples, and walnuts in a salad bowl. Add the remaining ingredients, toss gently but thoroughly, and serve at once.

GREEN SALAD WITH ORANGES

Here is a tantalizing salad to serve with roast pork, ham, poultry, or game on a fall Sunday.

Serves 4

6 cups torn salad greens (romaine, chicory, and Boston lettuce)
2 medium oranges, peeled, seeded, and sectioned (remove the white membrane)
1/4 cup very thin rings of mild white onion
12 pitted black olives
1/2 cup grapefruit sections (optional)
3/4 cup sliced avocado
1 tiny clove garlic
1/2 teaspoon salt
1-1/2 tablespoons freshly squeezed and strained lemon juice
1 teaspoon freshly squeezed and strained orange juice
3 tablespoons olive oil

Combine the salad greens, oranges, onion, olives, grapefruit, and avocado in a salad bowl. In a small bowl mash the garlic with the salt until smooth. Stir in the lemon and orange juices, then the oil. Pour over the salad. Toss gently but thoroughly and serve immediately.

GREEN SALAD WITH ORANGES AND CUCUMBER

An unlikely but surprisingly successful combination.

Serves 6

1 head Boston or Bibb lettuce, separated into leaves
4 medium oranges, peeled, seeded, and sliced
1/2 medium cucumber, peeled and sliced
1/2 medium red onion, thinly sliced and separated into rings
12 pitted black olives
1/3 cup olive oil or vegetable oil
2 tablespoons wine vinegar
1/4 teaspoon chili powder or to taste
Salt and freshly ground black pepper to taste

Line a shallow salad bowl with the lettuce leaves. Arrange the orange slices over the lettuce and top with the cucumber slices and onion rings. Garnish with the olives. In a small bowl beat together the oil, vinegar, chili powder, and salt and pepper with a fork or whisk until blended. Sprinkle evenly over the salad. Serve at once.

BUFFET-STYLE GREEN SALAD

The various ingredients of this salad are presented separately, making it possible for each guest to help himself to a selection of his choice.

Bring to the table a large salad bowl containing an assortment of greens, such as equal parts of romaine and leaf lettuce, with small amounts of Belgian endive and chicory, all torn into bite-size pieces. Surround with smaller bowls containing other foods to be added to the salad, such as pitted black and green olives, or pitted black olives stuffed with toasted slivered blanched almonds, sticks of Monterey Jack or Swiss cheese, or carrot sticks; marinated artichoke hearts, drained, or Artichokes, Asparagus, or Green Beans Vinaigrette, page 53; avocado cubes; croûtons (see page 27); freshly grated Parmesan cheese; crumbled crisp bacon; toasted halved almonds or filberts; toasted sesame seeds; and thinly sliced scallions. Toss the greens with French Dressing, page 138, and serve in individual salad bowls. Allow guests to help themselves to a selection of the other ingredients. You may offer a choice of dressings, but in my opinion a plain oil and vinegar dressing goes best with this salad.

Vegetable Salads

A pleasant alternative to a tossed green salad is one made with vegetables. It lends spark and variety to a winter menu and a refreshing note to a summer meal. A cooked vegetable salad may function either as an appetizer or side dish. It is an ideal choice for entertaining since it can be prepared in advance and kept in the refrigerator without wilting.

Vegetables selected for salad should be of good quality and as fresh as possible. Raw vegetables must be well washed, cold, crisp, and dry. Cooked vegetables must not be overdone but instead be rather firm. They should be drained immediately after cooking and will absorb their dressing better if dressed while warm.

COLE SLAW

Serves 6
1 medium head green cabbage
1 small mild white onion, finely
    chopped
3/4 cup Mayonnaise, page 146
Freshly squeezed and strained lemon
    juice to taste
2 teaspoons caraway seeds

Remove the outer leaves and hard core from the cabbage and discard. Shred the cabbage finely and combine with the onion in a salad bowl. Mix together the mayonnaise, lemon juice, and caraway seeds and pour over the cabbage and onion. Toss lightly but thoroughly. Taste and adjust the seasoning. Cover and chill before serving.

Variations French Dressing, page 138, Boiled Dressing, page 152, Sour Cream and Vegetable Dressing, page 157, or Sour Cream and Roquefort Dressing, page 158, may be substituted for the mayonnaise, lemon juice, and caraway seeds. Red cabbage or a combination of red and green cabbage may be used.

Vegetable Salads

LEBANESE CABBAGE SALAD

Many are the cole slaw haters, I among them, who have eagerly devoured the following delicious salad, a winter favorite in Lebanon.

Serves 4

2 cups finely shredded green cabbage
1/2 cup thinly sliced green pepper
1 small tomato, seeded and finely
    chopped
1/4 cup thinly sliced red or white
    onion or scallions
2 tablespoons finely chopped parsley
2 tablespoons finely chopped mint
1/4 cup olive oil
1/4 cup freshly squeezed and strained
    lemon juice
1 medium clove garlic, crushed
    (optional)
Salt to taste

Combine the cabbage, green pepper, tomato, onion, parsley, and mint in a salad bowl. Beat together the oil, lemon juice, garlic, and salt with a fork or whisk until well blended and pour over the vegetables. Toss gently but thoroughly and serve at once.

ARMENIAN SALAD

The Armenians have devised some of the finest salads in the world. Here is a popular summertime combination that often accompanies barbecued meat, chicken, or fish.

Serves 6

2 medium tomatoes, seeded and diced
1 medium green pepper, seeded, de-
    ribbed, and diced
1 medium cucumber, peeled, quartered
    lengthwise (cut out the seeds if too
    large and discard), and diced
1 cup sliced celery
2 scallions, finely chopped, including
    2 inches of the green tops
1/2 cup finely chopped parsley
2 tablespoons finely chopped mint, or
    1 tablespoon crushed dried mint
1/2 teaspoon ground cumin, or
    2 teaspoons crushed dried oregano
3 tablespoons olive oil
1 to 2 tablespoons freshly squeezed
    and strained lemon juice
Salt and freshly ground black pepper
    to taste
Romaine lettuce leaves

Combine the tomatoes, green pepper, cucumber, celery, scallions, and parsley in a bowl. Mix together the mint, cumin, olive oil, lemon juice, and salt and pepper and pour over the vegetables. Toss gently but thoroughly and serve over the lettuce leaves.

ARAB SALAD

After centuries of preparing and eating salads, Middle Easterners have developed countless delectable creations. In its many variations, the following is a favorite throughout the Arab world.

Serves 6

2 large tomatoes, seeded and diced
1 medium cucumber, peeled, quar-
    tered lengthwise (cut out the seeds
    if too large and discard), and diced
1 small green pepper, seeded, deribbed,
    and diced
1 medium avocado, peeled, pitted,
    and cubed
4 scallions, chopped, including
    2 inches of the green tops
6 radishes, diced
1/4 cup chopped parsley
1/4 cup chopped mint
1 small clove garlic
1/2 teaspoon salt
1/4 cup freshly squeezed and strained
    lemon juice
Freshly ground black pepper to taste
1/4 cup olive oil

Combine the tomatoes, cucumber, green pepper, avocado, scallions, radishes, parsley, and mint in a salad bowl. In a small bowl mash the garlic with the salt. Add the lemon juice and mix well. Sprinkle with the pepper and, using a fork or whisk, gradually beat in the oil until well blended. Pour the dressing over the vegetables and toss gently but thoroughly. Taste and adjust the seasoning. Serve at once.

✗ INDIAN CUCUMBER AND YOGURT SALAD

Serves 4

2 cups unflavored yogurt
4 scallions, finely chopped, including
    2 inches of the green tops
1 teaspoon ground cumin or to taste
1/2 teaspoon salt or to taste
2 medium cucumbers, peeled, quar-
    tered lengthwise (cut out the
    seeds if too large and discard),
    and thinly sliced

Combine the yogurt, scallions, cumin, and salt in a bowl. Stir in the cucumbers. Serve chilled.

Vegetable Salads

CUCUMBERS VINAIGRETTE

Serves 6
2 medium cucumbers, peeled and
    very thinly sliced
1/4 cup white wine vinegar
1/4 cup freshly squeezed and strained
    lemon juice
6 tablespoons olive oil
1 small clove garlic, crushed (optional)
1/2 teaspoon salt
Freshly ground black pepper to taste
Bibb or Boston lettuce leaves

Place the cucumbers in a bowl. Mix
together the remaining ingredients except the lettuce leaves and pour over
the cucumbers. Toss gently but thoroughly. Cover and refrigerate 1 hour,
occasionally turning the cucumbers
about in the dressing. Serve on the
lettuce leaves, sprinkled with the dressing. Or drain the cucumbers and serve
on an hors d'oeuvre tray, or use them
to garnish a salad plate.

CARROT AND CUCUMBER SALAD WITH YOGURT

Yogurt is a healthful food that has
played an important culinary role in
the Caucasus since very ancient times,
and for centuries Caucasians have been
addicted to raw vegetables and fruits,
possibly another reason for their good
health and longevity. This wholesome
and interesting salad comes from the
Caucasus, where salads are enjoyed not
only at lunch and dinner but for
breakfast as well.

Serves 4
4 medium carrots, peeled and grated
2 medium cucumbers, peeled, seeded
    (if necessary), and diced
1 cup unflavored yogurt
3 tablespoons freshly squeezed and
    strained lemon juice
3 tablespoons olive oil
Salt to taste
1/4 cup finely chopped dill or to taste

Combine the carrots and cucumbers in
a salad bowl. Beat the yogurt, lemon
juice, oil, and salt with a fork until
well blended. Stir in the dill. Pour over
the vegetables and mix thoroughly.
Taste and adjust the seasoning. Serve
chilled.

CUCUMBER AND ALMOND SALAD

Here is a distinctively delicious salad
to serve with seafood.

Serves 4
2 medium cucumbers, peeled, seeded
    (if necessary), and diced
1/3 cup ground toasted blanched
    almonds
1/4 cup olive oil
1 tablespoon freshly squeezed and
    strained lemon juice or to taste
1 to 2 cloves garlic, crushed
Salt and freshly ground black pepper
    to taste
Romaine lettuce leaves

Combine the cucumbers, almonds, oil,
lemon juice, garlic, and salt and pepper
in a bowl. Mix thoroughly. Taste and
adjust the seasoning. Cover and refrigerate until well chilled. Serve on the
lettuce leaves.

Variation A pinch of curry powder
and/or 1 teaspoon minced dill may be
added to this salad.

Vegetable Salads

MARINATED MUSHROOMS

Serves 6 to 8
1 pound small mushrooms
1 cup olive oil
3/4 cup freshly squeezed and strained
  lemon juice
1/4 cup white wine vinegar
1 small stalk celery, sliced
1 very small onion, thinly sliced
1 bay leaf
1 tablespoon salt
1-1/2 teaspoons black peppercorns
1/2 teaspoon ground coriander
3 quarts water

Wipe the mushrooms clean with a damp cloth. In an enameled or stainless steel saucepan combine the mushrooms with the remaining ingredients and bring to a boil. Boil 10 minutes. Remove from the heat and pour the mixture into a heatproof bowl. Allow to cool to room temperature, then cover and chill. These add an interesting note to an hors d'oeuvre tray.

TOMATO SALAD

Wonderful with steak or hamburger, but remember that in this or any other tomato salad the quality of the tomatoes will greatly affect results.

Serves 4
4 medium firm, ripe tomatoes, peeled
  and cut into thin vertical slices
1/4 cup French Dressing, page 138
1 tablespoon chopped basil or dill
1 tablespoon finely chopped chives or
  scallions
1 tablespoon chopped parsley

Arrange the tomatoes in overlapping rows on a serving dish. Combine the dressing with the herbs and spoon over the tomatoes just before serving.

Variation Omit the basil, chives, and parsley. Add a tiny clove of garlic, crushed, and 1/2 teaspoon crushed dried oregano to the dressing and mix well. Spoon over the tomatoes. Cover and chill at least 2 hours.

TOMATO AND ONION SALAD

A lively, cumin-scented Middle Eastern salad.

Serves 4
2 medium firm, ripe tomatoes, cut
  into vertical slices
1 medium mild onion, chopped, or
  4 scallions, chopped, including
  2 inches of the green tops
2 tablespoons finely chopped parsley
1/2 teaspoon ground cumin
3 tablespoons olive oil
1 tablespoon freshly squeezed and
  strained lemon juice or wine vinegar
1 medium clove garlic, crushed
  (optional)
Salt and freshly ground black pepper
  to taste

Combine the tomatoes, onion, and parsley in a salad bowl. Sprinkle with the cumin. Beat together the oil, lemon juice, garlic, and salt and pepper with a fork or whisk until well blended and pour over the salad. Toss gently but thoroughly and serve.

JAPANESE CUCUMBER AND TOMATO SALAD

Serves 4 to 6

2 medium cucumbers, peeled, cut in
    half lengthwise (cut out the seeds
    if too large and discard), and
    thinly sliced
2 medium tomatoes, seeded and cut
    into small pieces
1/2 cake deep-fried bean curd,
    thinly sliced
1 tablespoon soy sauce
1 tablespoon white wine vinegar
1 tablespoon crushed toasted sesame
    seeds, page 138
2 teaspoons sugar
1/2 teaspoon salt

Combine the cucumbers, tomatoes,
and fried bean curd in a salad bowl.
Mix together the remaining ingredients
until the sugar is dissolved. Pour over
the salad and toss gently but thoroughly. Taste and adjust the seasoning.
Cover and chill 1 hour before serving.

Note The deep-fried bean curd may
be purchased from Oriental food shops
and some supermarkets. Or the bean
curd may be purchased unfried, and
deep-fried at home in vegetable oil.

49

Vegetable Salads

AVOCADO AND TOMATO SALAD

Avocado has a remarkable affinity with tomato, as shown in the following fragrantly delicious Israeli combination.

Serves 4

2 medium ripe avocados, peeled, pitted, and diced
1 large firm, ripe tomato, seeded and diced
4 scallions, finely chopped, including 2 inches of the green tops
2 tablespoons finely chopped parsley
2 tablespoons finely chopped mint
2 tablespoons olive oil
2 tablespoons freshly squeezed and strained lemon juice
Salt and freshly ground black pepper to taste
12 pitted black olives

Combine the avocados, tomato, scallions, parsley, and mint in a salad bowl. Beat together the oil, lemon juice, and salt and pepper with a fork or whisk until well blended and pour over the vegetables. Toss gently but thoroughly and serve garnished with the olives.

AVOCADO SALAD GUATEMALA

An exciting choice for a luncheon entrée.

Serves 4

2 ripe avocados, peeled, pitted, and diced
2 large firm, ripe tomatoes, diced
3 hard-cooked eggs, diced
1 small mild onion, finely chopped
10 pimiento-stuffed olives
1/2 cup French Dressing, page 138
1/2 teaspoon chili powder or to taste
Lettuce leaves
6 slices bacon, cooked crisp and crumbled

Combine the avocados, tomatoes, eggs, onion, and olives in a bowl. Mix together the dressing and chili powder and pour over the salad. Toss gently but thoroughly. Serve on the lettuce leaves, sprinkled with the bacon.

GAZPACHO

This ancient dish of Spanish origin is a highly variable one and can be served in so many different ways, including as a salad, that it is difficult to assign it to a single course. In the modern Spanish cuisine there are at least 40 different recipes for *gazpacho*, ranging from thin liquid soups to thicker, more substantial creations that can function as main courses. The following Mexican version provides a wonderfully refreshing introduction to a summer meal.

Serves 6

1 cucumber, peeled, seeded (if necessary), and chopped
1 small mild red or white onion, finely chopped
1 medium avocado, peeled, pitted, and chopped
1 teaspoon crushed dried oregano
3 tablespoons olive oil
1-1/2 tablespoons wine vinegar
4 cups tomato juice
Salt and freshly ground black pepper or cayenne pepper to taste
Ice cubes
Thin slices of cucumber
2 limes, cut into wedges

Combine the cucumber, onion, avocado, oregano, oil, and vinegar in a bowl. Add the tomato juice and salt and pepper. Stir gently, cover, and refrigerate until thoroughly chilled. Just before serving stir lightly, then ladle the *gazpacho* into chilled individual bowls, adding an ice cube or two to each bowl. Garnish with the cucumber slices and accompany with the lime wedges.

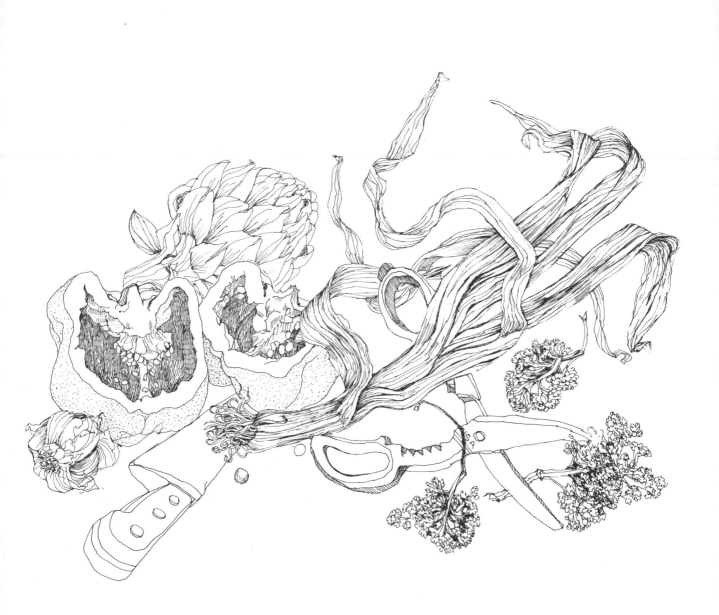

ARTICHOKES VINAIGRETTE

Serves 4 to 6
1-1/2 pounds tiny artichokes
1/4 cup French Dressing, page 138
1/8 teaspoon dry mustard

Remove any coarse outer leaves from the artichokes. Slice off the tops so that only 1 inch remains above the heart of the vegetable. Trim the stems. Cook in boiling salted water until tender. Test by pulling off a leaf. If it pulls off easily, the artichokes are done. Drain thoroughly.

Quarter the boiled artichokes and place them in a bowl. Blend together the dressing and mustard and pour over the artichokes. Cover and refrigerate several hours, stirring occasionally. Serve on lettuce leaves, toss in a green salad, or use to garnish a salad plate.

Note Two 10-ounce packages frozen artichoke hearts may be substituted for the fresh artichokes. Cook according to package directions.

Other cooked and cut vegetables, such as asparagus, green beans, zucchini, cauliflower, beets, and mushrooms may also be prepared in this manner. Garlic French Dressing or Lemon French Dressing, page 138, may be substituted for the above dressing.

GREEK ARTICHOKE SALAD

Serves 4 to 6
1-1/2 pounds tiny artichokes
4 scallions, finely chopped, including 2 inches of the green tops
1/4 cup olive oil
1/4 cup freshly squeezed and strained lemon juice
1/2 teaspoon crushed dried oregano
2 hard-cooked eggs, quartered (optional)

Prepare and cook the artichokes as described in the recipe for Artichokes Vinaigrette, preceding. Drain thoroughly. Quarter the boiled artichokes and place in a salad bowl. Add the scallions, oil, lemon juice, and oregano. Toss gently but thoroughly. Serve garnished with the quartered eggs, if you like.

Note Two 10-ounce packages frozen artichoke hearts may be substituted for the fresh artichokes. Cook according to package directions.

Vegetable Salads

JERUSALEM ARTICHOKE SALAD

An appetizing way of preparing this little-known and neglected vegetable.

Serves 4 to 6
1-1/2 pounds Jerusalem artichokes
6 tablespoons freshly squeezed and
    strained lemon juice
6 cups water
Boston lettuce leaves
1/4 cup olive oil
1 medium clove garlic, crushed
Salt and freshly ground black pepper
    to taste
2 tablespoons finely chopped parsley
1 scallion, finely chopped, including
    2 inches of the green tops

Pare the Jerusalem artichokes and place in a bowl of cold water to which 1 tablespoon of the lemon juice has been added. Combine 1 tablespoon of the remaining lemon juice with the water in a saucepan and bring to a boil. Drop in the drained artichokes and reduce the heat to low. Cover and simmer about 15 to 20 minutes or until the artichokes are tender but still somewhat firm. Drain and cool. Cut into thick slices and arrange on the lettuce leaves, which have been placed on a flat serving platter. Combine the oil and garlic in a small bowl. Stir to extract the garlic flavor, then discard the garlic. Add the remaining 4 tablespoons lemon juice and salt and pepper. Beat together with a fork until well blended. Stir in the parsley and scallions and pour over the artichokes. Serve chilled.

ASPARAGUS MIMOSA

Serves 6
2 pounds asparagus
2 hard-cooked eggs
1/2 cup French Dressing, page 138

Snap off the tough lower parts of the asparagus stalks. Tie the asparagus in bundles of about 10 to 12 stalks and drop them into a large saucepan of rapidly boiling salted water. Boil, uncovered, about 10 to 15 minutes or until just tender. Drain. Plunge into cold water and drain thoroughly. Place on a platter, cover, and chill. About 1 hour before serving, finely chop the egg whites and add to the dressing. Pour over the asparagus. Just before serving, force the egg yolks through a sieve directly onto the asparagus, leaving the tips uncovered.

Variation Place 4 slices crisp cooked bacon, crumbled, on a piece of waxed paper. Sieve the egg yolks over the bacon. Add 1 tablespoon minced parsley. Sprinkle over the dressed asparagus, leaving the tips uncovered.

CHINESE ASPARAGUS SALAD WITH WALNUTS

Serves 4

1-1/2 pounds young asparagus,
   trimmed and cut on the diagonal
   into 1-1/2-inch pieces
1/2 cup finely chopped walnuts
   (preferably freshly shelled)
1 tablespoon walnut or Oriental
   sesame oil
1 tablespoon white wine vinegar
2 tablespoons soy sauce
1 tablespoon sugar or to taste

Cook the asparagus in boiling water 3 minutes. Drain at once and run cold water over the asparagus. Drain and dry thoroughly.

Combine the remaining ingredients in a bowl. Mix until the sugar is dissolved. Add the asparagus and toss well. Cover and chill 1 hour before serving.

X ITALIAN RED BEAN SALAD

Serve this robust Sicilian salad as an hors d'oeuvre or as a luncheon main course.

Serves 4
1 20-ounce can red kidney beans, drained and rinsed
1/4 cup olive oil
2 tablespoons red wine vinegar
2 tablespoons freshly squeezed and strained lemon juice
1 medium clove garlic, crushed (optional)
1/2 teaspoon crushed dried oregano (optional)
Salt and freshly ground black pepper to taste
1/4 cup finely chopped sweet onion
2 tablespoons finely chopped parsley
8 slices Italian salami, cut in julienne
Chicory or escarole leaves
1 medium tomato, sliced (optional)
2 hard-cooked eggs, sliced (optional)

Place the beans in a bowl. Beat together the oil, vinegar, lemon juice, garlic, oregano, and salt and pepper with a fork or whisk until well blended. Pour over the beans. Cover and refrigerate several hours. One hour before serving, stir in the onion, parsley, and salami. Line a serving dish with the chicory leaves. Heap the beans in the center. Surround the beans with the tomato and egg slices.

Note Chick-peas or a combination of chick-peas and red kidney beans may be substituted for the beans. Drained canned tuna may be used instead of the salami.

X GREEN BEAN SALAD

Serves 4
2 quarts salted water
1 pound green beans, trimmed and cut into 2-inch pieces
1 small clove garlic
1/2 teaspoon salt or to taste
1/4 cup freshly squeezed and strained lemon juice
1/4 cup olive oil
Freshly ground black pepper to taste
1 medium tomato, seeded and chopped (optional)

Bring the salted water to a boil over high heat. Drop in the beans and boil, uncovered, about 10 minutes or until they are tender but still crisp. Drain the beans and keep them warm. Meanwhile, in a small bowl mash the garlic with the salt until smooth. Stir in the lemon juice, then the oil and pepper. Pour over the beans and toss lightly but thoroughly. Taste and adjust the seasoning, cover, and refrigerate until chilled. Just before serving, gently mix in the chopped tomato and taste again for seasoning.

Note Frozen green beans may be substituted for the fresh beans. Cook according to package directions, drain, and proceed as above.

FOUR BEAN SALAD

Serves 10 to 12

1 pound green beans, or
   1 10-ounce package frozen cut green beans
1 pound wax beans, or
   1 10-ounce package frozen cut wax beans
1 10-ounce package frozen small lima beans, or
   1 16-ounce can chick-peas, drained and rinsed
1 16-ounce can red kidney beans, drained and rinsed
1 medium green pepper, seeded, de-ribbed, and thinly sliced into rings
1 medium sweet red or white onion, cut crosswise in thin slices and separated into rings
1 cup French Dressing, page 138
1 medium clove garlic, crushed
2 tablespoons finely chopped parsley
2 teaspoons finely chopped tarragon, or 1/2 teaspoon crushed dried tarragon (optional)
2 teaspoons finely chopped basil, or 1/2 teaspoon crushed dried basil (optional)
Crisp salad greens

If using fresh green and wax beans, trim, cut, and cook the beans for about 10 minutes in 2 quarts boiling salted water, until tender but still crisp. If frozen, cook the beans according to package directions. Be careful not to overcook them; they should be just tender, not mushy. Combine all the beans, green pepper, and onion in a bowl. Mix together the dressing, garlic, parsley, tarragon, and basil and pour over the vegetables. Toss gently but thoroughly. Cover and refrigerate until chilled, stirring occasionally. Just before serving, stir again, then drain off the excess dressing. Turn the salad into a bowl that has been lined with the salad greens.

BEET SALAD

The following recipe is a popular way of preparing this vegetable in the Middle East. Even more interesting is the unusual variation with yogurt, which combines deliciously with beets.

Serves 4
2 tablespoons olive oil
1 tablespoon red wine vinegar
1 tablespoon freshly squeezed and
   strained lemon juice
1 medium clove garlic, finely chopped
Salt and freshly ground black pepper
   to taste
1 pound beets, cooked, peeled, and
   cut in julienne or diced
2 tablespoons finely chopped onion or
   scallions (white portions of scallions only)
2 tablespoons finely chopped parsley
Boston lettuce leaves

Combine the oil, vinegar, lemon juice, garlic, and salt and pepper and beat together with a fork or whisk until well blended. Place the beets, onion, and parsley in a bowl. Pour the dressing over them and toss lightly but thoroughly. Taste and adjust the seasoning. Cover and refrigerate several hours or overnight. Just before serving, stir gently and taste again for seasoning. Serve on the lettuce leaves. This is good with chicken, beef, or cold cuts.

Variation The beets may also be dressed with equal amounts of olive oil and lemon juice, salt, pepper, and minced parsley.

Beet Salad with Yogurt Variation Combine 2 tablespoons each olive oil and lemon juice. Add 1 cup unflavored yogurt and salt to taste and beat until well blended. Fold in the diced beets and mix well. Serve garnished with a border of sliced cooked beets and sprinkled with parsley.

BROCCOLI SALAD

Serves 4
1-1/2 pounds tender broccoli, or
   2 10-ounce packages frozen broccoli
1 small clove garlic
1/2 teaspoon salt or to taste
2 tablespoons freshly squeezed and
   strained lemon juice
Freshly ground black pepper to taste
3 tablespoons olive oil

If using fresh broccoli, trim and wash well. Cover and cook, heads up, in 1 inch boiling salted water 15 minutes or until tender. Drain and keep warm. Cook frozen broccoli according to package directions.

In a small bowl mash the garlic with the salt until smooth. Stir in the lemon juice, then the pepper and oil. Pour over the broccoli and toss gently but thoroughly. Taste and adjust the seasoning and serve.

CHINESE BROCCOLI SALAD

Serves 4

1 bunch tender broccoli
1 tablespoon Oriental sesame oil
1 tablespoon white wine vinegar
1 tablespoon soy sauce
1 tablespoon sugar or to taste
1 tablespoon toasted sesame seeds,
    page 138, or minced water
    chestnuts (optional)

Using a knife, separate the broccoli flower from the stems. Cut the flower part into small clusters. Remove the tough ends of the stems. Peel the stems, quarter lengthwise, and cut each quarter diagonally into approximately 2-inch pieces. Cook the broccoli in boiling salted water to cover 3 minutes. Drain at once and run cold water over the broccoli. Drain thoroughly and place in a salad bowl. Mix together the remaining ingredients until the sugar is dissolved. Pour over the broccoli and toss gently but thoroughly. Cover and chill 1 hour before serving.

CHINESE SNOW PEA, CAULIFLOWER, AND WATER CHESTNUT SALAD

Serves 4

8 ounces snow peas, trimmed and
    strings removed
1/2 head cauliflower, separated
    into flowerets
12 fresh water chestnuts, peeled,
    washed, and thinly sliced, or
    12 canned water chestnuts, rinsed,
    drained, and thinly sliced
1 tablespoon chopped pimiento
3 tablespoons vegetable oil
1/4 teaspoon Oriental sesame oil
1 tablespoon white wine vinegar
1 teaspoon sugar
1/2 teaspoon salt or to taste
1 tablespoon toasted sesame seeds,
    page 138

Cook the snow peas in boiling salted water about 1 minute or until almost tender. Drain and set aside. Cook the cauliflower in boiling salted water about 5 minutes or until tender but still firm. Drain.

Combine the snow peas, cauliflower, water chestnuts, and pimiento in a salad bowl. Mix together the remaining ingredients until well blended and pour over the vegetables. Toss gently but thoroughly. Taste and adjust the seasoning. Serve chilled.

Variations One-half cup diced cooked shrimp or julienne-cut ham may be added to the vegetables.

Instead of the above dressing, you may use 3 tablespoons vegetable or olive oil, 1 tablespoon each freshly squeezed and strained lemon juice and white wine vinegar, 1 tiny clove garlic, crushed, 1 tablespoon toasted sesame seeds, and salt to taste.

MASKED CAULIFLOWER SALAD

A lovely salad, perfect for a special meal.

Serves 6

1 head cauliflower, trimmed
2 medium avocados, peeled, pitted, and mashed
2 medium ripe tomatoes, peeled, seeded, and diced
1 mild white onion, finely chopped
Salt
6 tablespoons olive oil
3 tablespoons wine vinegar
1/4 teaspoon freshly ground black pepper
1 small clove garlic, crushed
2 tablespoons freshly grated Parmesan cheese (optional)

Place the cauliflower in a kettle of boiling salted water to cover. Cover and simmer about 25 minutes or until just tender. Do not overcook. Drain. Cover and chill. Combine the avocados, tomatoes, and onion in a bowl. Add salt to taste and mix together until well blended. Place the chilled cauliflower on a serving plate. Beat together the oil, vinegar, 1/4 teaspoon salt, pepper, and garlic with a fork or whisk until thoroughly mixed. Spoon over the cauliflower. Frost the cauliflower with the avocado and tomato mixture. Sprinkle with the cheese, if you wish, and serve.

Variation Instead of frosting the cauliflower with the avocado, tomato, and onion mixture, you may cover it with Avocado-Shrimp Mayonnaise, page 149, and garnish with slices of avocado and tomato, a few cooked shrimp, and pitted black olives. Omit the cheese.

EGGPLANT SALAD

There seems to be no end to dishes made with eggplant in the Armenian repertory. The recipe described below ranks as a classic.

Serves 4

1 large eggplant (about 2 pounds)
About 3 tablespoons freshly squeezed and strained lemon juice or more
2 scallions, finely chopped, including 2 inches of the green tops
2 tablespoons finely chopped parsley
1 tablespoon finely chopped dill
About 2 tablespoons olive oil
Salt and freshly ground black pepper to taste
4 cherry tomatoes, halved
8 pitted black olives

Cut the stem and hull from the top of the eggplant and discard. Using a long-handled fork, prick the skin of the eggplant in several places, then insert the fork tines into it until secure and broil over charcoal or a gas flame, turning it frequently until the flesh is very soft and the skin charred. (The eggplant may instead be broiled in an electric oven. Place it on a baking sheet and broil 4 inches from the heat about 25 minutes, turning it to char evenly on all sides.) It is important that the eggplant be thoroughly cooked inside; otherwise it will have a bitter taste, rendering the dish inedible. When the eggplant is cool enough to handle, gently squeeze it to remove the bitter juices. Peel off the skin, remove the badly charred spots, and slit the eggplant open. Scoop out the seeds and discard. Place the eggplant flesh in a bowl, immediately pour the lemon juice over it, and chop it finely. Add the scallions, parsley, and dill. Season with the oil and salt and pepper, adding more lemon juice or oil if needed. Mix gently but thoroughly, cover, and chill. Serve garnished with the tomatoes and olives.

SALATA MESHWIYA
(Roasted Tomato and
Green Pepper Salad)

An immense favorite in Tunisia and neighboring countries, where it is traditionally served as an hors d'oeuvre or as an accompaniment to broiled or fried fish.

Serves 4
4 medium firm, ripe tomatoes
4 medium green peppers
1/3 cup finely chopped mild onion
3 tablespoons freshly squeezed
    and strained lemon juice
1-1/2 teaspoons salt
Freshly ground black pepper to taste
Cayenne pepper to taste (optional)
3 tablespoons olive oil
12 black olives (preferably Greek
    olives)

Arrange the tomatoes and peppers on a baking sheet. Roast them in a preheated 400° oven 15 minutes, turning them frequently so they color evenly on all sides. Remove the tomatoes, but continue roasting the peppers about 15 minutes longer, turning them occasionally. Meanwhile, peel and quarter the tomatoes. Remove and discard the seeds and excess juice. Finely chop the tomato pulp. When the peppers are evenly colored and soft, remove them

from the oven. Skin them, cut out the stems and white membrane, and discard the seeds. Finely chop the peppers. Combine the lemon juice, salt, black pepper, and cayenne in a serving bowl. Stir to dissolve the salt. Add the tomatoes, green peppers, and onion and toss lightly but thoroughly. Taste and adjust the seasoning. Sprinkle with the oil and garnish with the olives. Serve chilled.

CORN SALAD

Serves 4
2 cups cooked corn kernels
1/2 cup diced green pepper
1/4 cup diced pimiento
1 medium tomato, peeled, seeded,
    and diced
1 tablespoon finely chopped parsley
1/4 cup Garlic French Dressing,
    page 138
Lettuce leaves
4 slices bacon, cooked crisp and
    crumbled
Thinly sliced red onion rings

Combine the corn, green pepper, pimiento, tomato, and parsley in a bowl. Add the dressing and toss gently but thoroughly. Taste and adjust the seasoning. Serve on the lettuce leaves, garnished with the bacon and onion rings.

LENTIL SALAD ✗

Serves 4
1 quart water
2 teaspoons salt
1 cup lentils
1/2 cup finely chopped onion
2 scallions, finely chopped, including
    2 inches of the green tops
1 medium clove garlic, finely chopped
2 tablespoons finely chopped parsley
6 tablespoons olive oil or vegetable oil
2-1/2 tablespoons red wine vinegar
Salt, freshly ground black pepper,
    and cayenne pepper to taste
2 hard-cooked eggs, cut crosswise in
    thin slices (optional)
1 small sweet onion, cut crosswise in
    thin slices and separated into rings
Parsley sprigs

In a heavy saucepan bring the water and 2 teaspoons salt to a boil over high heat. Add the lentils, reduce the heat to low, partially cover, and simmer about 25 minutes or until the lentils are just tender, not mushy. Drain thoroughly and place in a salad bowl. Stir in the onion, scallions, garlic, and parsley. Beat together the oil, vinegar, and salt, pepper, and cayenne with a fork or whisk until well blended. Pour over the salad and toss lightly but thoroughly with a fork. Cover and chill. Serve garnished with the egg slices, onion rings, and parsley sprigs.

Vegetable Salads

SALAD OF BOILED VEGETABLES

Substantial and colorful, this Middle Eastern dish can fill the role of both a vegetable and a salad. Other vegetables can be substituted for those listed below.

Serves 6
2 medium potatoes
3 small zucchini, trimmed and cut
    crosswise into 1/2-inch-thick slices
1 large beet
1/2 head small cauliflower, trimmed
4 ounces green beans, trimmed and
    cut into 2-inch lengths
3/4 cup Lemon French Dressing
    or Garlic French Dressing, page 138

Cook each vegetable separately in boiling salted water until tender but still somewhat firm. Drain well. Peel and dice the potatoes and beet. Separate the cauliflower into flowerets. Arrange the vegetables in separate groups on a large serving platter. Sprinkle with the dressing and serve chilled.

GADO-GADO
(Indonesian Vegetable Salad)

Serves 6
2 tablespoons peanut oil or
    vegetable oil
1/3 cup finely chopped onion
1 large clove garlic, finely chopped
1/2 cup chunk-style peanut butter
1 teaspoon brown sugar
1/2 teaspoon salt
1 small fresh red chili pepper, finely
    chopped, or Tabasco sauce to
    taste
1-1/2 teaspoons grated lemon peel
1/2 teaspoon *trasi*   (optional)
3/4 cup coconut milk, page 103
1 cup green beans, trimmed, cut
    into 1-1/2-inch lengths, and
    cooked
1 cup shredded cabbage, cooked
    5 minutes
2 medium tomatoes, seeded and diced
2 medium cucumbers, peeled, cut
    lengthwise in half (cut out the
    seeds if too large and discard),
    and thinly sliced crosswise
2 hard-cooked eggs, coarsely chopped

In a heavy skillet heat the oil over moderate heat. Add the onion and garlic and sauté 3 minutes, stirring constantly. Add the peanut butter, sugar, salt, red pepper, lemon peel, *trasi*, and coconut milk and cook over low heat a few minutes until smooth, stirring frequently. Remove from the heat and set aside.

Arrange the beans, cabbage, tomatoes, and cucumbers on a serving platter. Sprinkle with the chopped eggs. Pour over the peanut sauce and serve.

Note This salad can also be made with other vegetables such as potatoes, spinach, bean sprouts, and carrots. The tomatoes may be omitted.

Trasi, or shrimp paste, is a strong-flavored seasoning, brown in color and salty in flavor. Sold in small packages in stores specializing in Indonesian or Philippine foodstuffs and in some Oriental markets.

POTATO SALADS

Out of the vast range of potato salads I have selected a classic French recipe and several unusual ones to provide an exciting change from standard fare in this category.

✗ FRENCH POTATO SALAD

Serves 6

2 pounds small potatoes, boiled
   in jackets
2 tablespoons dry white wine
2 tablespoons chicken broth
1/2 cup French Dressing, page 138
2 tablespoons finely chopped shallots
   or scallions
2 tablespoons finely chopped parsley

Peel and slice the potatoes about 1/4 inch thick while still warm and place them in a mixing bowl. Combine the wine and broth and pour over the potatoes. Toss gently and let stand until the liquid is absorbed. Mix together the dressing, shallots, and parsley and pour over the potatoes. Toss lightly but thoroughly. Taste and adjust the seasoning. Serve lukewarm or chilled.

Herbed French Potato Salad Variation
One teaspoon each minced tarragon and basil and 1/2 teaspoon minced thyme (or 1/4 teaspoon crushed dried thyme) may be added with the parsley.

CHEESE AND POTATO SALAD

Two favorite Swiss foods are featured in this rich, creamy salad, perfect for a buffet or outdoor meal.

Serves 6
1 pound potatoes, boiled in jackets
1/4 cup French Dressing, page 138
8 ounces Emmenthal or Gruyère
   cheese, diced
1/2 cup diced celery heart
2 scallions, finely chopped, including
   2 inches of the green tops
4 hard-cooked eggs
3 tablespoons finely chopped parsley
2 slices bacon, cooked crisp and
   crumbled
About 1/2 cup Mayonnaise, page 146
1 teaspoon Dijon-style mustard
Salt and freshly ground black pepper
   to taste
Lettuce leaves

Peel and dice the potatoes while still warm. Sprinkle with the dressing. Toss gently and allow to cool. In a mixing bowl combine the potatoes, cheese, celery heart, scallions, 3 of the eggs, chopped, 2 tablespoons of the parsley, and bacon. Mix the mayonnaise with the mustard and add to the salad. Mix gently but thoroughly. Season with the salt and pepper. Cover and chill. To serve, mound the salad in a bowl lined with the lettuce. Chop the remaining egg finely and mix with the remaining 1 tablespoon parsley. Sprinkle over the salad.

PAPAS A LA HUANCAINA
(Peruvian Potato Salad)

Serves 6
8 ounces Muenster cheese, freshly
   grated
4 hard-cooked egg yolks
2 mashed, seeded mild green chili
   peppers, or
   1 teaspoon chili powder
1/4 cup olive oil
1 cup heavy cream
1 tablespoon freshly squeezed and
   strained lemon juice
1/4 cup finely chopped onion
Salt and freshly ground black pepper
   to taste
2 pounds small new potatoes, cooked
   and peeled
Bibb or Boston lettuce leaves
3 hard-cooked eggs, quartered
6 pimiento-stuffed olives or black
   olives

In a bowl combine the cheese, egg yolks, and chilies and beat vigorously with a wooden spoon. Gradually add the oil, then the cream and lemon juice, beating constantly. Add the onion and salt and pepper and blend thoroughly. Taste and adjust the seasoning. Arrange the potatoes on a serving platter. Frost with the cheese sauce. Garnish with the lettuce leaves, eggs, and olives. Serve at room temperature or chilled.

Note One-half teaspoon turmeric may be added with the cheese. Cheddar cheese may be substituted for the Muenster.

SPANISH HOT POTATO SALAD

Serves 6

6 medium potatoes, boiled in jackets
6 slices bacon
1 small mild onion, finely chopped
1 medium green pepper, seeded, deribbed, and finely chopped
1 tablespoon all-purpose flour
1/2 teaspoon crushed dried oregano
1/8 teaspoon ground cumin or to taste
1-1/2 cups light cream
3 tablespoons grated Gruyère cheese
1/4 cup dry sherry
4 hard-cooked egg yolks, crumbled
1 pimiento, finely chopped
2 tablespoons wine vinegar
1 tablespoon finely chopped parsley
2 tablespoons finely chopped walnuts

Peel and cube the potatoes while still warm and place them in a salad bowl; set aside.

In a heavy skillet cook the bacon over moderate heat until crisp, turning frequently. Drain, reserving 3 tablespoons of the drippings. Crumble the bacon and set aside. Return the reserved drippings to the skillet. Add the onion and green pepper and sauté over moderate heat until soft but not browned, stirring frequently. Add the flour, oregano, and cumin and cook over low heat, stirring, until the flour begins to turn a pale gold. Gradually add the cream, stirring constantly until smooth. Add the cheese and mix well. Simmer until the sauce is thickened and hot. Add the sherry, egg yolks, pimiento, vinegar, and parsley and mix well. Taste and adjust the seasoning. Remove from the heat and pour over the potatoes. Toss gently but thoroughly. Sprinkle with the reserved crumbled bacon and walnuts and serve immediately.

GERMAN POTATO SALAD WITH SOUR CREAM

Serves 6
6 medium potatoes, boiled in jackets
1/4 cup white wine vinegar
2 teaspoons sugar
1 teaspoon salt
1/4 teaspoon freshly ground black pepper
1/4 teaspoon dry mustard (optional)
1 pint sour cream
1 cup peeled and thinly sliced cucumber (optional)
Paprika

Peel and slice the potatoes while still warm and place them in a mixing bowl. Combine the vinegar, sugar, salt, pepper, and mustard and mix well. Add the sour cream and cucumber and mix again. Pour over the potatoes and toss gently but thoroughly. Taste and adjust the seasoning. Place in a serving dish and sprinkle with the paprika.

RUSSIAN POTATO AND BEET SALAD

Serves 4
4 medium potatoes
1 large beet
1/2 cup peeled, seeded (if necessary), and diced cucumber, or 1/4 cup diced dill pickle
2 hard-cooked eggs, coarsely chopped
1/3 cup pitted black olives, sliced
2 scallions, finely chopped, including 2 inches of the green tops
1/4 cup chopped walnuts
1/4 cup olive oil or vegetable oil
2 tablespoons wine vinegar
Salt and freshly ground white pepper to taste
1/2 cup sour cream

Cook the potatoes and beet separately in boiling salted water until just tender. Drain, peel while still warm, and dice. Combine the diced potatoes and beet with the cucumber, eggs, olives, scallions, and walnuts in a mixing bowl. Sprinkle with the oil, vinegar, and salt and pepper and toss gently but thoroughly. Add the sour cream and toss again. Taste and adjust the seasoning. Cover and chill before serving.

GREEK POTATO SALAD

Serves 6
6 medium potatoes, boiled in jackets
2 large mild onions, thinly sliced
1/2 cup olive oil
1/2 cup freshly squeezed and strained lemon juice
1/2 teaspoon crushed dried oregano
Salt and freshly ground black pepper to taste
8 black olives (preferably Greek olives) (optional)

Peel and cube the potatoes while still warm. Combine the cubed potatoes and onions in a salad bowl. Add the oil, lemon juice, oregano, and salt and pepper and toss gently but thoroughly. Taste and adjust the seasoning. Serve, garnished with the olives if you like.

Vegetable Salads

MEXICAN HOT VEGETABLE SALAD

Serves 6

Dressing
5 slices bacon, cut into 1/2-inch
  pieces and cooked crisp
1/4 teaspoon chili powder
Salt and freshly ground black pepper
  to taste
3 tablespoons wine vinegar
1/3 cup water
1 teaspoon sugar

1 cup warm peeled and cubed
  cooked potatoes
1 cup warm cut cooked green beans
3/4 cup warm cooked cauliflower
  flowerets
1/2 cup warm cooked sliced carrots
1/2 cup warm cooked green peas
Lettuce leaves
2 medium tomatoes, cut into wedges
1 medium cucumber, peeled and sliced

To make the dressing, cook the ingredients over low heat until hot, stirring to dissolve the sugar. Keep warm over a low flame.

Combine the potatoes, beans, cauliflower, carrots, and peas in a bowl. Add the hot dressing and toss gently but thoroughly. Taste and adjust the seasoning. Transfer to a heated serving dish lined with the lettuce leaves. Garnish with the tomatoes and cucumber and serve at once.

PERSIAN SALAD

Serves 4
1 large beet, cooked, peeled, and diced
1 4-ounce jar marinated artichokes,
  drained and chopped
2 hard-cooked eggs, chopped
2 tomatoes, quartered, seeded, and
  chopped
2 medium cucumbers, peeled, seeded
  (if necessary), and diced
2 medium dill pickles, diced
8 pitted black olives, chopped
1/4 cup chopped parsley
3/4 cup French Dressing, page 138

Combine all the ingredients except the dressing in a salad bowl. Add the dressing and toss gently but thoroughly. Taste and adjust the seasoning. Chill before serving.

GUACAMOLE

One of the most famous of all Mexican specialties, *guacamole* has become quite popular in the United States. A dish with multiple virtues, it may be eaten as a dip accompanied with tortilla chips, as a sauce for *tacos* and *tostadas*, as a dressing for sliced tomatoes, and as a salad heaped on lettuce.

Makes about 1-1/2 cups
1 large ripe avocado, peeled, pitted,
  and mashed
1 small tomato, peeled, seeded, and
  finely chopped
1-1/4 teaspoons olive oil
1 tablespoon freshly squeezed and
  strained lemon juice
1/2 teaspoon chili powder
1 small clove garlic, crushed, or
  1/2 teaspoon garlic powder
2 tablespoons finely chopped onion, or
  1 teaspoon onion powder
Dash cayenne pepper
1 teaspoon salt or to taste

Combine all the ingredients and mix thoroughly. Taste and adjust the seasoning. Serve chilled.

HUMMUS BI TAHINI
(Chick-Pea Purée)

This Middle Eastern favorite is excellent served as an appetizer or as an accompaniment to broiled fish or meat. *Tahini* is a nutty-flavored paste made from crushed sesame seeds and can be purchased from Middle Eastern groceries, gourmet shops, and some supermarkets.

Serves 4

1 15-ounce can chick-peas
3 tablespoons freshly squeezed and
    strained lemon juice
Up to 3 tablespoons cold water
3 tablespoons *tahini*
1 small clove garlic, crushed
3/4 teaspoon salt or to taste
Paprika
1 tablespoon olive oil
Parsley or mint sprigs
Radish roses

Drain the chick-peas, removing the transparent shell, if desired. Reserve 1/4 cup of the chick-peas for garnish. Put the lemon juice, water, *tahini*, garlic, salt, and chick-peas in that order in the container of an electric blender. Cover and blend until smooth and creamy. (Alternately, press the chick-peas through a sieve or food mill or pound them in a mortar. Add the crushed garlic and pound or mash together until well mixed. Gradually beat in the lemon juice, water, *tahini*, and salt until the mixture is smooth and creamy.) Taste and adjust the seasoning. Spread the purée on a shallow serving dish, cover, and chill. Just before serving, mix a little paprika with the oil and drizzle over the surface of the purée. Garnish with the reserved chick-peas, parsley sprigs, and radish roses. Serve as a salad or as an appetizer, accompanied by Arab bread, if available, or French bread.

BABA GHANNOUJ
(Eggplant Purée)

Not so well known as the preceding recipe but equally delicious.

Serves 4

1 medium eggplant (about 1 pound)
3 tablespoons freshly squeezed and
    strained lemon juice
3 tablespoons *tahini*, preceding
1 clove garlic, crushed
1 teaspoon salt or to taste
Pomegranate seeds
Chopped parsley

Broil and peel the eggplant as described in the recipe for Eggplant Salad, page 62. Place the eggplant pulp, lemon juice, *tahini*, garlic, and salt in the container of an electric blender. Cover and blend until smooth and creamy. (Alternately, place the eggplant pulp in a bowl and mash it thoroughly with a fork. Gradually beat in the lemon juice, *tahini*, garlic, and salt until the mixture is smooth and creamy.) Taste and adjust the seasoning. Spread the eggplant purée on a shallow serving dish, cover, and chill. Just before serving, garnish the top with the pomegranate seeds and parsley. Serve as a salad or appetizer, accompanied by Arab bread, if available, or French bread.

Vegetable and Fruit Salads

Some of the most glorious salads ever devised are artful concoctions of vegetables and fruits, whose enchantment lies in their unexpected contrasts and combinations of taste. The following recipes, with their unusual blend of ingredients and flavors, may seem odd at first glance, but once you have tried them salad making will gain a new dimension.

APPLE, BEET, AND WALNUT SALAD

This Persian salad is a fascinating amalgam of tastes and textures.

Serves 4

2 tart apples, peeled, cored, and chopped
2 beets, cooked, peeled, and chopped
6 stalks celery, sliced
1/3 to 1/2 cup chopped walnuts (preferably freshly shelled)
1/4 cup olive oil
2 tablespoons wine vinegar
2 tablespoons freshly squeezed and strained orange juice
Salt and freshly ground black pepper to taste
1 small clove garlic, crushed (optional)
Chicory leaves

Combine the apples, beets, celery, and walnuts in a bowl. Beat together the oil, vinegar, orange juice, salt and pepper, and garlic with a fork or whisk until well blended and pour over the salad. Toss gently but thoroughly. Taste and adjust the seasoning. Serve over the chicory leaves.

Vegetable and Fruit Salads

APPLE, CARROT, AND RADISH SALAD

Here is a crunchy, relish-like preparation that goes well with lamb, pork, or veal.

Serves 4
2 tart, crisp green apples, pared and cored
2 medium carrots, peeled
10 medium radishes, peeled if desired
1/4 cup finely chopped mild onion
2 tablespoons finely chopped parsley
1/4 cup olive oil
1 tablespoon freshly squeezed and strained lemon juice or to taste (optional)
Salt to taste

Cut the apples, carrots, and radishes into small dice. Combine them in a salad bowl with the onion and parsley. Sprinkle with the oil, lemon juice, and salt. Mix thoroughly and adjust the seasoning. Serve chilled.

AUSTRIAN APPLE AND POTATO SALAD

Serves 6
1 pound tart green apples, peeled, cored, and diced
1 pound potatoes, cooked, peeled, and diced
1/4 cup olive oil
1/4 cup white wine vinegar
Salt and freshly ground black pepper to taste
2 beets, cooked, peeled, and sliced
2 hard-cooked eggs, sliced

Combine the apples and potatoes in a bowl. Beat together the oil, vinegar, and salt and pepper with a fork or whisk until well blended. Pour over the apples and potatoes. Toss gently but thoroughly. Taste and adjust the seasoning. Serve garnished with the beets and eggs.

PINEAPPLE-STUFFED TOMATO SALAD

An inspired invention from Hawaii.

Serves 6
6 small, firm ripe tomatoes, peeled and chilled
1-1/2 cups shredded fresh pineapple, chilled
1/2 cup chopped roasted peanuts
2 tablespoons Lemon French Dressing, page 138
Pinch ground ginger (optional)
1 teaspoon salt
Lettuce leaves

Make 1/2-inch caps by cutting across the stem ends of the tomatoes without cutting all the way through. These caps will later serve as lids. Using a spoon, scoop out the inside of each tomato, leaving a 1/4-inch-thick shell. Chop the tomato pulp coarsely (discard the seeds) and combine with the pineapple and peanuts. Add the dressing, ginger, and salt and mix gently but thoroughly. Spoon the mixture into the tomatoes and cover with the tops. Serve on individual salad plates lined with the lettuce leaves.

EMIR'S PEARLS

Worthy of an emir, this Middle Eastern creation tastes as sublime as it looks.

Serves 4

4 medium oranges, peeled and
    thinly sliced
1 small sweet white onion, cut into
    very thin rings
16 pitted black olives
2 tablespoons olive oil
2 tablespoons freshly squeezed and
    strained lemon juice
Salt to taste
Mint sprigs

Arrange the orange slices on a serving platter. Top with the onion rings and olives. Sprinkle with the oil, lemon juice, and salt. Serve chilled, garnished with the mint.

77

Vegetable and Fruit Salads

ENSALADA DE NOCHE BUENA
(Mexican Christmas Eve Salad)

In Mexico this festive dish would include *jícama*, a bulb-shaped root vegetable not always available in the United States.

Serves 6
1 large beet, cooked, peeled, and
   chopped
1 cup cubed fresh pineapple
1 *jícama* or tart apple, peeled and
   sliced (core the apple)
2 oranges, peeled and sectioned
   (remove the seeds and white
   membrane)
2 bananas, peeled and sliced
1/2 cup Lemon French Dressing,
   page 138
1/2 cup chopped raw or roasted peanuts
Pomegranate seeds (optional)

Combine the beet, pineapple, *jícama*, oranges, and bananas in a salad bowl. Add the dressing and toss lightly but thoroughly. Sprinkle with the peanuts and pomegranate seeds and serve.

Note The ingredients of this salad are sometimes arranged over a bed of lettuce, with French dressing or mayonnaise served on the side.

JÍCAMA SALAD WITH SALAMI AND CHEESE

Serves 4
3 cups julienne-cut *jícama* (preceding)
   or tart apple
1/2 cup julienne-cut Italian salami
1/2 cup julienne-cut Swiss cheese
1/2 cup French Dressing, page 138
Romaine lettuce leaves
Thinly sliced green pepper rings
Freshly grated Parmesan cheese
Finely chopped chives or scallions

Combine the *jícama*, salami, and Swiss cheese in a bowl. Add the dressing and toss gently but thoroughly. Cover and chill. To serve, mound the salad in a bowl lined with the lettuce. Garnish with the green pepper rings and sprinkle with the Parmesan cheese and chopped chives.

CANARY ISLAND SALAD

A delightfully discordant combination.

Serves 4
4 bananas, peeled
3 oranges, peeled and sectioned (remove the seeds and white membrane)
1 sweet red pepper, seeded, deribbed, and cut into strips
3 tablespoons olive oil
1 tablespoon freshly squeezed and strained lemon juice
1 tablespoon finely chopped mild onion
2 teaspoons finely chopped mint
1/4 cup freshly shredded coconut

Halve the bananas lengthwise, then crosswise, making 16 pieces. Combine the bananas, oranges, and red pepper in a salad bowl. Beat together the oil, lemon juice, onion, and mint with a fork or whisk until well blended and pour over the salad. Cover and refrigerate 1 hour, stirring occasionally. Serve sprinkled with the coconut.

Variation You may substitute Curry Fruit French Dressing, page 138, for the above dressing.

SALADE CATALANE

This extraordinary concoction was devised by the French painter Henri de Toulouse-Lautrec, whose keen interest in good food led him to lavish as much care upon the artistic creations in his kitchen as those in his studio.

Serves 6

1 large potato, cooked, peeled, and cubed
8 ounces chestnuts, cooked, peeled, and quartered
2 pounds beets, cooked, peeled, and diced
1/2 cup thinly sliced celery
2 heads Belgian endive, sliced
1 large sweet apple, peeled, cored, and chopped
2 bananas, peeled and sliced
1/2 cup julienne-cut Gruyere or Swiss cheese
1/4 cup chopped walnuts
About 1 cup French Dressing, page 138, or Mayonnaise, page 146

In a large salad bowl combine all the ingredients except the dressing. Add the dressing and toss lightly but thoroughly. Taste and adjust the seasoning. Serve chilled.

PORTUGUESE SALAD

Serves 4

2 green peppers, seeded, deribbed, and thinly sliced
2 medium tomatoes, peeled, seeded, and cut into wedges
1 medium cucumber, peeled and thinly sliced
1 medium mild red onion, cut lengthwise in half and thinly sliced
1 large tart apple, peeled, cored, and thinly sliced
1/2 cup olive oil
1/4 cup freshly squeezed and strained lime or lemon juice
1 small clove garlic, crushed
Salt and freshly ground black pepper to taste
8 chestnuts
Romaine lettuce leaves
2 hard-cooked eggs, cut into wedges
Pimiento strips

Combine the green peppers, tomatoes, cucumber, onion, and apple in a bowl. Beat together the oil, lime juice, garlic, and salt and pepper with a fork or whisk until well blended and pour over the vegetable mixture. Cover and refrigerate 1 hour.

Meanwhile, slit the chestnuts halfway around with a sharp knife without cutting through the meat. Place in a pan and bake in a preheated 450° oven 15 minutes. Remove the chestnuts from the oven and, while still hot, peel off their outer shells and inner membranes. Cover the chestnuts with salted water and simmer, uncovered, 20 minutes or until tender. Drain and cool them, then force them through a sieve.

Serve the vegetable mixture over the lettuce leaves, sprinkled with the sieved chestnuts and garnished with the eggs and pimiento strips.

ROMAN SALAD

Serves 6

4 ounces lean cooked ham or prosciutto, cut in julienne
2 medium potatoes, cooked, peeled, and cut in julienne
4 ounces Swiss or Gruyère cheese, cut in julienne
1 medium tart green apple, peeled, cored, and cut in julienne
1 small mild red or white onion, finely sliced
About 1/2 cup Mayonnaise, page 146
Salt and freshly ground black pepper to taste

Combine the ham, potatoes, cheese, apple, and onion in a bowl. Add the mayonnaise and toss gently but thoroughly. Taste and adjust the seasoning. Serve chilled.

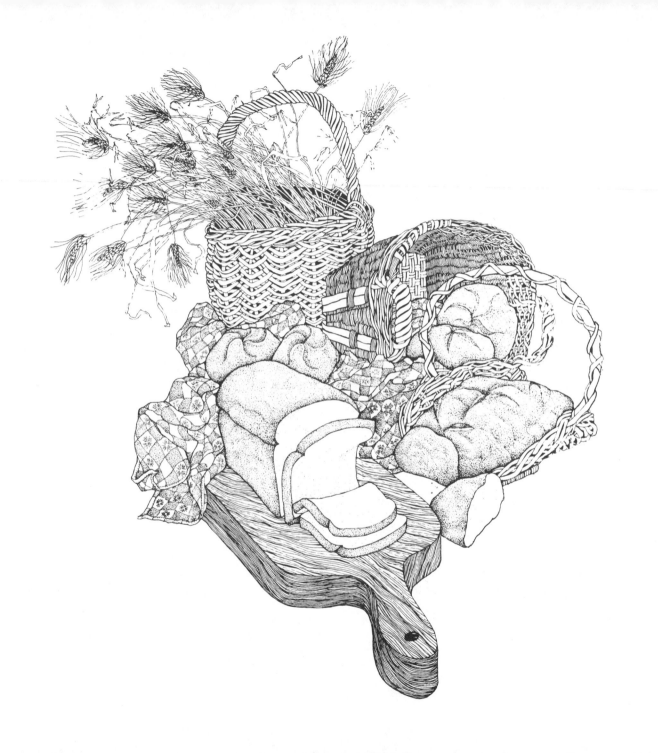

Bread, Cereal, and Pasta Salads

The salads in this category are hearty, economical, and palatable. Both pasta and rice salads can be prepared in advance and actually improve if allowed to chill several hours, giving flavors a chance to intermingle and mellow. Be careful not to overcook pasta or rice. When done they should be, as the Italians say, *al dente*, offering a slight resistance to the bite.

FATTOUSH
(Bread Salad)

Here is a deservedly popular peasant salad from Syria and Lebanon.

Serves 4
2 cups bite-size pieces toasted Arab
    or French bread
1 medium cucumber, peeled, seeded
    (if necessary), and diced
2 medium tomatoes, quartered,
    seeded, and diced
1 small green pepper, seeded,
    deribbed, and diced (optional)
1 small sweet onion, finely
    chopped, or
    4 scallions, finely chopped,
    including 2 inches of the
    green tops
1/3 cup finely chopped parsley
1/3 cup finely chopped mint, or
    1 tablespoon crushed dried mint
1/3 cup olive oil
1/3 cup freshly squeezed and
    strained lemon juice
1 medium clove garlic, crushed
    (optional)
Salt to taste

Combine the bread, cucumber, tomatoes, green pepper, onion, parsley, and mint in a salad bowl. Mix together the oil, lemon juice, garlic, and salt and pour over the salad. Toss gently but thoroughly. Taste and adjust the seasoning. Serve at once.

Note Chopped romaine lettuce leaves may be used instead of the cucumber or in addition to it. Minced coriander or thyme is sometimes added with the parsley, and sour pomegranate juice may replace the lemon juice.

Italian Bread Salad Variation Combine 4 cups cubed stale or lightly toasted Italian or French bread, 1 small cucumber, peeled and sliced, 2 medium tomatoes, cut into wedges, 1 small Bermuda onion, finely sliced, and 1 tablespoon chopped basil. Mix together 5 tablespoons olive oil, 2 tablespoons wine vinegar or to taste, 1 small clove garlic, crushed (optional), and salt and freshly ground black pepper to taste and pour over the salad. Toss and serve. Wedges of hard-cooked eggs and/or anchovy fillets are sometimes included in this salad.

ENSALADA CHALUPA
COMPUESTA
(Tortilla Sandwich Salad)

This hot Mexican luncheon salad is built on a crisp tortilla. Crab or chicken may be substituted for the shrimp.

Serves 4
1/4 cup vegetable oil
4 corn tortillas
Iceberg lettuce leaves
4 cups shredded iceberg lettuce
1 20-ounce can refried beans
1 cup shredded Monterey Jack or
    Cheddar cheese
12 ounces shrimp, cooked, shelled,
    deveined, and marinated 2 hours
    in Lemon French Dressing,
    page 138
Guacamole, page 72
Thinly sliced green pepper rings
Thinly sliced onion rings
Pitted black olives
Tomato wedges or cherry tomatoes,
    halved

In a large, heavy skillet heat the oil over moderate heat. Add the tortillas, one at a time, and fry until golden brown and crisp, about 2 minutes on each side. Line 4 dinner plates with the lettuce leaves and top each with 1/2 cup of the shredded lettuce. Set aside. Heat the refried beans. Place the fried tortillas on a cookie sheet and cover each with the hot beans. Sprinkle with the cheese and broil until the cheese melts.

Arrange the filled tortillas on top of the shredded lettuce on the plates. Sprinkle each with 1/2 cup of the remaining shredded lettuce. Cover with a layer of the shrimp and top with the guacamole. Garnish with the green pepper rings, onion rings, olives, and tomato wedges. Serve at once.

TABBOULI
(Cracked Wheat Salad)

Tabbouli is the unquestioned star of Lebanese salads and a national passion.

Serves 4
1 cup fine bulghur (cracked wheat)
1 medium mild onion, finely chopped,
    or
    4 scallions, finely chopped, includ-
    ing 2 inches of the green tops
1-1/2 cups finely chopped parsley
    (preferably Italian parsley)
1/4 cup finely chopped mint, or
    1 tablespoon crushed dried mint
1/4 cup olive oil
1/4 cup freshly squeezed and strained
    lemon juice
Salt to taste
Romaine lettuce hearts
2 medium tomatoes, chopped or
    sliced
Green pepper rings (optional)

Soak the bulghur in cold water to cover about 20 minutes. Drain and squeeze out as much moisture as possible with your hands. Combine the bulghur, onion, parsley, and mint in a bowl. Sprinkle with the oil, lemon juice, and salt and mix thoroughly. Taste and adjust the seasoning. Cover and chill. To serve, mound the salad in the center of a serving platter. Decorate with the romaine lettuce hearts, tomatoes, and green pepper rings. Use the romaine to scoop up the salad.

Note One-half cup each seeded and finely chopped tomato, cucumber, and green pepper may be added.

CURRIED RICE SALAD WITH SHRIMP

A distinctive, exotically spiced salad for a special luncheon or supper.

Serves 4

2 cups cold cooked long-grain white rice
1 medium green pepper, seeded, deribbed, and thinly sliced
1 whole canned pimiento, cut in strips
8 ounces cooked shrimp, diced
2 tablespoons chopped parsley
2 tablespoons chopped scallions (include 2 inches of the green tops)
1/2 cup olive oil
1/3 cup white wine vinegar
1 tablespoon freshly squeezed and strained lemon juice
1 medium clove garlic, crushed
1/2 teaspoon curry powder
Salt and freshly ground black pepper to taste
Crisp salad greens
Green pepper rings
Tomato wedges

Combine the rice, green pepper, pimiento, shrimp, parsley, and scallions in a salad bowl. Beat together the oil, vinegar, lemon juice, garlic, curry powder, and salt and pepper with a fork or whisk until well blended and pour over the salad. Toss gently but thoroughly. Taste and adjust the seasoning. Cover and chill. Serve garnished with the salad greens, green pepper rings, and tomato wedges.

HOT RICE SALAD

Serves 6

2 cups chicken broth
1 small clove garlic stuck on a food pick
1/2 bay leaf
1 cup long-grain white rice
2 tablespoons grated mild onion
1/4 cup French Dressing, page 138
1 cup diced cooked chicken
1 cup diced cooked shrimp
4 ounces mushrooms, sliced
1/4 cup diced pimiento
1/4 cup pitted black olives, sliced
1/3 cup toasted slivered blanched almonds
Salt and freshly ground black pepper to taste
Leaf lettuce leaves
Mayonnaise, page 146

In a heavy saucepan bring the chicken broth, garlic, and bay leaf to a boil over high heat. Stir in the rice. Reduce the heat to low, cover, and simmer about 20 minutes or until the liquid in the pan is completely absorbed and the rice is tender but still somewhat firm to the bite. Remove from the heat. Lift out the garlic and bay leaf and discard. Gently stir in the onion and the dressing. Add the chicken, shrimp, mushrooms, pimiento, olives, almonds, and salt and pepper. Toss lightly but thoroughly. Taste and adjust the seasoning. Return to the heat and cook just until heated through. Turn out on a serving platter lined with the lettuce leaves. Pass a bowl of the mayonnaise.

RICE AND BEET SALAD

This is a gratifying French salad, excellent either as a substantial appetizer or as a main course.

Serves 4
2 cups cold cooked long-grain white rice
2 cups peeled and diced cooked beets
1/4 cup finely chopped shallots or scallions
1/2 cup French Dressing, page 138
1 cup Herb Mayonnaise, page 148, or more French dressing
1/4 cup diced cooked green beans or peas
1/4 cup diced cooked carrots
1/2 cup diced cooked lean beef, chicken, or shrimp
Green or black olives
Sliced hard-cooked eggs
Watercress or parsley sprigs

Combine the rice, beets, and shallots in a bowl. Add the dressing and toss gently but thoroughly. Taste and adjust the seasoning. Cover and refrigerate at least 12 hours. Close to serving time, fold in the mayonnaise, green beans, carrots, and beef. Taste for seasoning. Serve garnished with the olives, eggs, and watercress.

DANISH MACARONI SALAD

Serves 4 to 6
8 ounces elbow macaroni
4 hard-cooked eggs
1/2 teaspoon dry mustard
1 teaspoon salt
1/3 cup Mayonnaise, page 146
2/3 cup sour cream
1 canned pimiento, diced
1 cup finely chopped Danish boiled ham
2 tablespoons finely chopped parsley or dill

Cook the macaroni as directed on the package. Drain well and set aside to cool. In a salad bowl mash the yolks of 2 of the eggs (discard the egg whites or reserve for some other use). Add the mustard and salt to the yolks. Gradually mix in the mayonnaise, then fold in the sour cream. Add the pimiento, ham, and cooled macaroni and toss gently but thoroughly. Taste and adjust the seasoning. Cover and chill. Garnish with the remaining 2 eggs cut in slices, and sprinkle with the parsley.

MACARONI SALAD WITH SALAMI AND CHEESE

Serves 6
8 ounces small shell macaroni
2 cups julienne-cut Swiss cheese
12 slices Genoa-style salami, cut in julienne
1/2 cup finely diced celery heart
1/2 cup finely diced green pepper
1 cup pitted black olives, sliced
1/4 cup thinly sliced scallions (include 2 inches of the green tops)
Salt and freshly ground white pepper to taste
1/4 teaspoon crushed dried oregano (optional)
About 1 cup Garlic French Dressing, page 138
Crisp lettuce leaves
1 cup cherry tomatoes, halved

Cook the macaroni as directed on the package. Drain well and cool. Combine the cooled macaroni, cheese, salami, celery, green pepper, olives, and scallions in a large bowl. Sprinkle with the salt and pepper and oregano. Add the dressing and toss gently but thoroughly. Taste and adjust the seasoning. Cover and refrigerate several hours until well chilled, stirring 2 or 3 times. Serve on the lettuce leaves, garnished with the tomatoes.

Meat, Poultry, and Seafood Salads

Substantial enough to fill the function of a main course, the following salads make satisfying luncheon or supper entrées especially suitable for hot weather. Supplemented with good bread, a beverage, and dessert, many of them provide easy yet impressive meals for special occasions. Served in smaller portions, some are equally effective as appetizers.

BEEF AND POTATO SALAD

This French salad is an excellent way of utilizing leftover beef and makes a fine luncheon or buffet dish.

Serves 6
1-1/2 pounds lean boiled or braised
   beef, thinly sliced
1 large mild onion, cut into thin
   slices and separated into rings
1-1/2 cups cooked green beans or
   broccoli (optional)
French Dressing, page 138
Lettuce leaves or watercress
French Potato Salad, page 67
3 hard-cooked eggs, quartered
2 medium tomatoes, cut into wedges
1/4 cup chopped mixed herbs (parsley, chives, basil, and tarragon)

Place the beef, onion, and green beans in separate bowls. Cover each with the dressing and let marinate at least 2 hours in the refrigerator. Just before serving, arrange the marinated beef and onion rings in overlapping rows on a large platter. Surround with the lettuce leaves. Garnish with the marinated beans, potato salad, eggs, and tomatoes. Spoon a little dressing over the eggs and tomatoes and sprinkle the salad with the herbs.

Meat, Poultry, and Seafood Salads

MEXICAN BEEF SALAD WITH ORANGES

The sweet-sour piquancy of the orange and the mild pungency of the onion create an ideal counterpoint to the roast beef.

Serves 6

1-1/2 pounds very tender lean roast beef, cut in julienne
1 medium Bermuda onion, cut crosswise in very thin slices and separated into rings
2 medium oranges, peeled, seeded, and thinly sliced
1 cup French Dressing, page 138
Lettuce leaves
3 fresh red chili peppers, seeded and cut into strips
Coriander or parsley sprigs

Combine the beef, onion, and oranges in a bowl. Add enough dressing to cover and allow to marinate at least 2 hours in the refrigerator. To serve, line a platter with the lettuce leaves. Arrange the beef, onion rings, and orange slices on top. Sprinkle with the dressing remaining in the bowl. Decorate with the pepper strips and the coriander sprigs.

GERMAN VEAL SALAD

Serves 4

1 pound cubed cooked veal
1-1/2 cups peeled and cubed cooked potatoes
1 large tart apple, peeled, cored, and diced
2 sweet pickled gherkins, chopped
1/2 cup French Dressing, page 138
About 1/2 cup Mayonnaise, page 146
1 teaspoon Dijon-style mustard
Lettuce leaves
2 hard-cooked eggs, sliced
Sliced pickled beets
2 tablespoons finely chopped chives or parsley

Combine the veal, potatoes, apple, and pickled gherkins in a bowl. Cover with the French dressing and let marinate 2 hours in the refrigerator. Mix together the mayonnaise and the mustard. Add to the salad and toss gently but thoroughly. Taste and adjust the seasoning. Cover and chill several hours.

To serve, mound the salad in the middle of a platter. Garnish with the lettuce leaves, sliced hard-cooked eggs, and pickled beets and sprinkle with the chives.

SALPICÓN
(Cuban Meat Salad)

Though not indispensable, the oregano is an agreeable addition to the following hearty and nourishing combination.

Serves 6

1-1/2 cups julienne-cut cold very tender lean roast beef
1-1/2 cups julienne-cut cold roast chicken
3 cups peeled and cubed cooked potatoes
1 large green pepper, seeded, deribbed, and chopped
1 cup chopped romaine lettuce hearts
1/4 cup finely chopped mild onion
2 canned pimientos, drained and chopped
1/2 cup pimiento-stuffed olives, sliced
1 to 1-1/2 cups French Dressing, page 138
1 teaspoon crushed dried oregano (optional)
Watercress or lettuce leaves
3 hard-cooked eggs, quartered

In a salad bowl combine the beef, chicken, potatoes, green pepper, lettuce, onion, pimientos, and olives. Add the dressing and oregano and toss lightly but thoroughly. Serve garnished with the watercress and eggs.

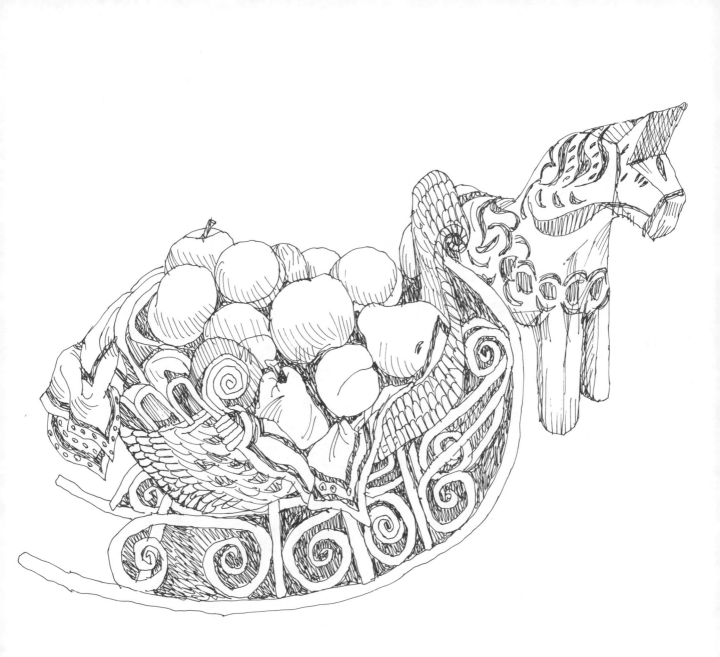

HAM AND POTATO SALAD

Here is a useful recipe for turning left-over ham into an appetizing dish.

Serves 4
1-1/2 cups cubed cooked lean ham
2 cups peeled and cubed cooked
    potatoes
3 hard-cooked eggs, chopped
1/2 cup sliced peeled cucumber
1/3 cup thinly sliced celery
3 tablespoons finely chopped mild
    onion
3 tablespoons finely chopped green
    pepper
1/2 cup or more Italian Dressing,
    page 143
Lettuce leaves

Combine the ham, potatoes, eggs, cu-cumber, celery, onion, and green pep-per in a bowl. Add the dressing and toss gently but thoroughly. Cover and refrigerate several hours until well chilled. Serve on the lettuce leaves.

HAM AND CHEESE SALAD

A suitable salad for a casual lunch, supper, or picnic.

Serves 4 to 6
1 small mild red or white onion
4 ounces lean cooked ham, cut in
    julienne
4 ounces Emmenthal or Gruyère
    cheese, cut in julienne
1 large green pepper, seeded, deribbed,
    and cut in julienne
1/4 cup olive oil
2 tablespoons wine vinegar
Salt and freshly ground black pepper
    to taste
Romaine or iceberg lettuce leaves

Cut the onion crosswise in very thin slices and separate into rings. Cover with ice water and refrigerate 2 hours. Drain well and place in a bowl. Add the ham, cheese, green pepper, oil, vinegar, and salt and pepper. Toss lightly but thoroughly. Taste and ad-just the seasoning. Serve chilled over the lettuce leaves.

Note A cooked, peeled, and diced po-tato may be added to this salad.

BRAZILIAN HAM AND FRUIT SALAD

Serves 4
4 ounces thinly sliced prosciutto or
    cooked lean ham, cut in julienne
1 medium mango, peeled, seeded,
    and slivered
1 medium tart apple, peeled, cored,
    and slivered
1 large banana, peeled and diced
2 cups diced fresh pineapple
1 cup seedless grapes
About 1/4 cup Mayonnaise, page 146
1/4 cup heavy cream, whipped
Lettuce leaves
Strawberries

In a bowl combine the prosciutto, mango, apple, banana, pineapple, and grapes. Mix together the mayonnaise and whipped cream. Add to the salad and toss lightly but thoroughly. Taste and adjust the seasoning. Serve on the lettuce leaves, garnished with the strawberries.

Meat, Poultry, and Seafood Salads

MIDDLE EASTERN TONGUE SALAD

Serves 4

1 fresh beef or calf's tongue (about 2 pounds), trimmed of fat and gristle
2 medium onions
2 medium carrots, peeled
2 stalks celery with leaves
1-1/2 teaspoons salt
6 whole black peppercorns
Lettuce leaves
1/2 cup thinly sliced scallions or mild onion
1/2 cup finely chopped parsley
1/4 cup olive oil
2 tablespoons freshly squeezed and strained lemon juice
1 tablespoon wine vinegar
1 large clove garlic, crushed (optional)
Salt and freshly ground black pepper to taste
2 hard-cooked eggs, sliced
2 medium tomatoes, sliced
8 black olives

Scrub the tongue and rinse thoroughly under cold running water. Place it in a pot with the onions, carrots, and celery. Cover with boiling water and add the salt and peppercorns. Cook about 2 hours or until tender. Remove the tongue from the pot and allow it to cool slightly, then skin and slice it.

Line a serving platter with the lettuce leaves. Arrange the tongue slices in overlapping rows on top and sprinkle with the scallions and parsley. Beat together the oil, lemon juice, vinegar, garlic, and additional salt and pepper with a fork or whisk until well blended. Spoon over the tongue. Garnish with the eggs, tomatoes, and olives. Serve immediately.

ROSSOLYE
(Estonian Mixed Salad)

This salad makes a fine addition to a buffet. Or serve it as an appetizer or first course, accompanied with vodka if you like. The Lithuanian version incorporates more vegetables and is known as *vinegretas*.

Serves 6

1 pound cooked ham or boiled beef, trimmed of fat and cut into 1/2-inch dice
1 fillet *matjes* herring, drained and cut into 1/4-inch dice
3 medium potatoes, cooked, peeled, and cut into 1/2-inch dice
1 large tart apple, peeled, cored, and cut into 1/2-inch dice
1 or 2 sour dill pickles, quartered lengthwise and cut into 1/4-inch dice
1 small mild onion, finely chopped (optional)
2 hard-cooked eggs, finely chopped
1 cup sour cream
1 to 2 tablespoons sharp prepared mustard or to taste
1 tablespoon white wine vinegar (optional)
1 teaspoon sugar
Salt to taste
3 medium beets, cooked, peeled, and sliced
2 hard-cooked eggs, sliced

Combine the meat, herring, potatoes, apple, pickle, onion, and finely chopped eggs in a large bowl. In a small bowl mix together the sour cream, mustard, vinegar, sugar, and salt until well blended. Add to the salad and toss gently but thoroughly. Taste and adjust the seasoning. Mound the salad on a serving platter. Garnish with the sliced beets and hard-cooked eggs. Serve chilled.

SALADE OLIVIER

This famous salad, also known as *salade russe*, was named after its creator, the French chef of Tsar Nicholas II.

Serves 4

1 whole chicken breast, cooked and
    cooled
2 medium potatoes, cooked, peeled,
    and diced
3/4 cup green peas, cooked
2 hard-cooked eggs, chopped
1/4 cup finely chopped onion or
    scallions (include 2 inches of
    the green tops of the scallions)
2 tablespoons sliced pitted green
    olives
1/4 cup chopped sour dill pickle
1/4 cup finely chopped celery heart
Salt and freshly ground black pepper
    to taste
1-1/2 cups Mayonnaise, page 146, or
    1 cup mayonnaise and 1/2 cup
    sour cream
Freshly squeezed and strained lemon
    juice to taste
1 tablespoon capers, drained
1 tablespoon finely chopped dill
6 whole pitted green or black olives
1 hard-cooked egg, cut into wedges
1 medium tomato, cut lengthwise
    into eighths
Boston lettuce leaves (from the heart)

Remove and discard the skin and bones of the chicken. Cut the meat into small cubes or strips and place in a bowl. Add the potatoes, peas, chopped eggs, onion, sliced olives, pickle, celery, salt and pepper, mayonnaise, and lemon juice. Toss gently to blend. Taste and adjust the seasoning. Mound the salad in the middle of a serving platter. Sprinkle with the capers and dill. Garnish with the olives, egg, tomato, and lettuce leaves. Serve chilled.

✗ KOREAN CHICKEN SALAD

Serves 4

1 3-pound chicken
1/3 cup dry sherry
1/3 cup soy sauce
1 teaspoon sugar
1 teaspoon finely chopped ginger
    root, or
    1/4 teaspoon powdered ginger
1/4 teaspoon ground dried red chili
    pepper
3 tablespoons peanut or vegetable oil
2 cups shredded iceberg or romaine
    lettuce
3/4 cup bean sprouts
3/4 cup thinly sliced celery
1/3 cup chopped blanched almonds
1-1/2 tablespoons sesame seeds

Cut the chicken meat from the bones and into bite-size pieces. Marinate 3 to 4 hours in a mixture of the sherry, soy sauce, sugar, ginger, and chili pepper. Drain, reserving the marinade.

In a heavy skillet heat the oil over moderate heat. Add the chicken and sauté until golden brown, stirring frequently. Reduce the heat to low, cover, and simmer 10 to 15 minutes or until the chicken is tender, sprinkling with some of the reserved marinade if the chicken seems dry. Remove from the heat and cool.

Combine the chicken with the remaining ingredients in a salad bowl and toss lightly but thoroughly. Taste and adjust the seasoning and serve.

CHICKEN SALAD PLATE

Here is an attractive way of serving a perennial favorite.

Serves 6

3 cups diced cooked chicken
1-1/2 cups diced cooked potatoes
1/2 cup diced cooked jumbo shrimp
  (optional)
1 cup diced peeled and seeded
  cucumber
1/2 cup very thinly sliced celery heart
1 cup Curry Mayonnaise, page 148
1 teaspoon finely chopped chives
1 teaspoon finely chopped parsley
Freshly squeezed and strained lemon
  juice to taste
Lettuce leaves
Green Bean Salad, page 56
1 small mild red or white onion,
  sliced into thin rings
3 hard-cooked eggs, quartered
1 medium tomato, cut into wedges
Pitted black olives

Combine the chicken, potatoes, shrimp, cucumber, and celery in a bowl. Mix together the mayonnaise, chives, parsley, and lemon juice. Add to the salad and toss gently but thoroughly. Taste and adjust the seasoning. Cover and chill. Line a serving platter with the lettuce leaves. Heap the chicken mixture in the center. Garnish with the green beans, onion, eggs, tomato, and olives.

Note Mayonnaise, page 146, mixed with 1/2 teaspoon crushed dried oregano, or Herb Mayonnaise, page 148, may be substituted for the curry mayonnaise.

Variation Omit the green beans and onion. Sprinkle the chicken with 1/3 cup chopped salted peanuts, cashews, or macadamias. Garnish with the eggs, tomato, olives, and 1 medium avocado, peeled, pitted, and sliced. Sprinkle with minced chives or scallions.

TURKEY SALAD WITH MUSHROOMS

Leftover turkey need not be a depressant!

Serves 4

3 cups cubed cooked turkey
1-1/2 cups sliced mushrooms
1 cup thinly sliced celery
1/3 cup pimiento-stuffed olives, sliced
1 tablespoon finely chopped onion or
  scallions
1/2 cup Lemon French Dressing,
  page 138
1/3 to 1/2 cup Curry Mayonnaise,
  page 148
1/2 teaspoon salt or to taste
Lettuce leaves
2 hard-cooked eggs, sliced
1/4 cup chopped salted roasted
  peanuts, cashews, or macadamias

Combine the turkey, mushrooms, celery, olives, and onion in a bowl. Add the dressing and allow to marinate 1 hour in the refrigerator, stirring the mixture several times. Add the mayonnaise and salt and toss gently but thoroughly. Taste and adjust the seasoning. Cover and chill. To serve, line a salad bowl with the lettuce leaves. Spoon in the turkey salad. Garnish with the eggs and sprinkle with the nuts.

DUCK SALAD WITH ORANGES AND WALNUTS

Serves 4

3 cups julienne-cut lean roast duck
1 small Bermuda onion, very thinly
    sliced
About 1/2 cup Lemon French
    Dressing, page 138
Grated rind of 1 orange
1 tablespoon butter
1/4 teaspoon garlic salt
1/4 cup coarsely chopped walnuts
3 medium oranges, peeled, seeded,
    and thinly sliced
Lettuce leaves

Combine the duck and onion in a bowl. Mix together the dressing and orange rind and pour over the duck and onion. Cover and refrigerate at least 2 hours, stirring occasionally. Meanwhile, in a small skillet heat the butter over moderate heat. Add the garlic salt and walnuts and sauté until the nuts turn golden brown, stirring frequently.

Close to serving time, combine the oranges with the duck and onion and toss gently but thoroughly, adding more dressing if needed. Taste and adjust the seasoning. Serve over the lettuce leaves, sprinkled with the sautéed nuts.

Meat, Poultry, and Seafood Salads

SALADE NIÇOISE

This appetizing and colorful Mediterranean specialty is made in numerous variations and is a great favorite on the Riviera. Served with a loaf of French or Italian bread and, if you wish, a glass of rosé wine, it will calm a starving man and delight a gourmet.

Serves 6 to 8

12 ounces green beans, trimmed, cooked, and cut into 1-1/2-inch lengths
4 medium tomatoes, quartered
1 cup French Dressing, page 138
1 head Boston lettuce, torn into bite-size pieces
1/2 recipe French Potato Salad, page 67
1 8-ounce can chunk-style tuna or salmon, drained
4 hard-cooked eggs, peeled and quartered
8 anchovy fillets
1/2 cup black olives (preferably Greek or Italian olives)
2 tablespoons finely chopped herbs (parsley, chives, tarragon, and basil)

Sprinkle the beans and tomatoes with a few spoonfuls of the dressing and set aside. Line a large, shallow bowl with the lettuce leaves. Sprinkle with about 1/4 cup of the dressing. Arrange the potato salad, beans, and tuna on top of the lettuce. Garnish with the tomatoes, eggs, anchovies, and olives. Pour the remaining dressing over the salad, sprinkle with the herbs, and serve.

Variation Line a serving platter with the lettuce leaves. Arrange the beans, tomatoes, 1 green pepper, seeded, deribbed, and thinly sliced, and 1 cup thinly sliced celery in a decorative pattern on top of the lettuce. Place small chunks of tuna here and there around the edge. Crisscross anchovy fillets over the tuna chunks. Garnish with the olives. Sprinkle the salad with Garlic French Dressing, page 138, and serve.

GREEK SALAD

This extravaganza could turn a stoic into an epicurean!

Serves 4
1 small head romaine lettuce
Greek Potato Salad, page 71
12 sprigs watercress or rocket leaves
    (arugula)
1 medium cucumber, peeled and sliced
2 medium tomatoes, sliced lengthwise
6 scallions, thinly sliced, including
    2 inches of the green tops
6 radishes, thinly sliced
1 small green pepper, seeded, deribbed, and thinly sliced into rings
1 avocado, peeled, pitted, and sliced
About 1 cup French Dressing,
    page 138
2 small beets, cooked, peeled, and sliced
4 anchovy fillets
12 black olives (preferably Greek olives)
8 ounces fresh or frozen shrimp, cooked
4 ounces feta cheese
1 teaspoon crushed dried oregano

Discard the outer leaves from the lettuce. Line a large serving platter with a few of the largest leaves and mound the potato salad in the center. Shred the remaining lettuce leaves and strew them and the watercress sprigs over and around the potato salad. Pile the cucumber, tomatoes, scallions, radishes, green pepper, and avocado in layers over the lettuce, sprinkling each layer with a little of the dressing. Garnish the entire surface of the mound with the beets, anchovies, olives, shrimp, and cheese. Sprinkle with the oregano, cover, and chill. Just before serving, pour the remaining dressing evenly over the salad. Crusty Greek bread, Armenian *peda* bread, or hot garlic toast go well with this salad.

CAPPON MAGRO
(Genoese Fish and Vegetable Salad)

The bounty of land and sea are artistically combined in this colorful and highly decorative Italian salad. A magnificent dish for a cold buffet.

Serves 8

Sauce
1/4 slice white bread, trimmed of crust
4 tablespoons wine vinegar
2 tablespoons parsley leaves
1 tiny clove garlic, peeled
1-1/2 teaspoons pine nuts
1 teaspoon capers
1 anchovy fillet
1 hard-cooked egg yolk
4 pitted green olives, sliced
1/2 cup olive oil
Salt and freshly ground pepper to taste

10 tablespoons olive oil
3 tablespoons wine vinegar
Salt and freshly ground black pepper
    to taste
1/2 head cauliflower, separated
    into flowerets and cooked
1 cup diced cooked green beans

1 cup diced cooked carrots
1 cup peeled and diced cooked beets
1 cup peeled and diced cooked
    potatoes
2 tablespoons freshly squeezed and
    strained lemon juice
1 cup flaked cooked codfish or
    haddock
1/2 cup cooked lobster meat
12 shrimp, cooked and peeled
1 9-ounce package frozen artichoke
    hearts, cooked
3 slices dry white bread, trimmed of
    crusts
1 small clove garlic, halved
1 tablespoon cold water
12 pimiento-stuffed olives
8 anchovy fillets
4 hard-cooked eggs, quartered

To make the sauce, place the bread in the container of an electric blender. Add 1 tablespoon of the vinegar, the parsley, garlic, pine nuts, capers, anchovy, egg yolk, and olives. Turn on the motor and gradually add the remaining 3 tablespoons vinegar and the oil while blending. Season with salt and pepper. Set aside. (If you have no blender, combine all the ingredients except the oil in a mortar and pound together, gradually adding the oil.)

Mix together 5 tablespoons of the oil, 2 tablespoons of the vinegar, and salt and pepper. Marinate the cauliflower, green beans, carrots, beets, and potatoes separately in the oil and vinegar dressing. Mix together the remaining 5 tablespoons oil with the lemon juice and additional salt and pepper. Marinate the codfish, lobster, shrimp, and artichoke hearts separately in the lemon and oil dressing. Rub the bread slices with the garlic and place them on a serving platter. Combine the water and remaining 1 tablespoon vinegar, add salt to taste, and sprinkle over the bread slices. Spoon some of the sauce over the bread. Reserve the shrimp, olives, anchovies, and 2 of the eggs for garnish. Layer the remaining foods over the bread slices to form a pyramid. Spoon the remaining sauce over the pyramid. Decorate the entire surface of the salad with the reserved shrimp and olives pierced with picks. Garnish the base with the reserved 2 hard-cooked eggs and anchovies.

SHELLFISH SALADS

Shellfish is a universally popular delicacy. The following shellfish salads are party-perfect and can provide an outstanding main course for a special luncheon.

ITALIAN SHRIMP AND POTATO SALAD

Serves 4

1 pound large shrimp, cooked, shelled, deveined, and coarsely chopped
2 cups peeled and cubed cooked potatoes
2 hard-cooked eggs, coarsely chopped
2 tablespoons sliced pitted black olives
1/4 cup Mayonnaise, page 146
1 tablespoon freshly squeezed and strained lemon juice
1/2 teaspoon crushed dried oregano
Salt and freshly ground black pepper to taste
Lettuce leaves
2 ripe medium tomatoes, cut into wedges

Combine the shrimp, potatoes, eggs, and olives in a bowl. Mix together the mayonnaise, lemon juice, oregano, and salt and pepper. Add to the salad and toss lightly but thoroughly. Cover and chill. Serve over the lettuce leaves, garnished with the tomatoes.

BRAZILIAN SHRIMP SALAD

Sensuous and beguiling, spicy and original, this is the sort of dish the girl from Ipanema might concoct.

Serves 4

2 bunches spinach
1-1/2 pounds medium shrimp, cooked, shelled, and deveined
1-1/4 cups very thinly sliced celery
1-1/4 cups julienne-cut green pepper
6 scallions, thinly sliced, including 2 inches of the green tops
1/4 cup finely chopped coriander or parsley (optional)
3/4 cup olive oil
3/4 teaspoon grated lime rind
1/4 cup freshly squeezed and strained lime juice
1 teaspoon sugar
3/4 teaspoon ground cumin
1/4 to 1/2 teaspoon crushed dried red chili pepper
Salt to taste
3 medium slightly underripe bananas, peeled and cut diagonally in 1-inch slices
1/2 cup chopped salted peanuts or shredded fresh coconut
Lime wedges

Wash the spinach thoroughly under cold running water. Remove the stems. Dry the spinach leaves, break them into bite-size pieces, and set aside. In a large bowl combine the shrimp, celery, green pepper, scallions, and coriander. In a small bowl mix together the oil, grated lime rind, lime juice, sugar, cumin, crushed red pepper, and salt. Pour over the salad. Toss gently but thoroughly. Taste and adjust the seasoning. Cover and chill 1 hour. To serve, line 4 individual plates with the spinach leaves. Mound the shrimp mixture on the spinach. Surround with the banana slices. Sprinkle with the peanuts and garnish with the lime wedges.

MEXICAN SHRIMP SALAD

Often served as an appetizer in Mexico, this salad makes an equally tempting main course. If you do not care for hot foods, you may omit the jalapeño chilies, which are very hot indeed.

Serves 4
1 pound large shrimp, cooked, shelled, deveined, and coarsely chopped
1 small white mild onion, finely chopped
3/4 cup olive oil
1/4 cup freshly squeezed and strained lemon juice
Salt and freshly ground black pepper to taste
1 large ripe tomato, peeled, seeded, and diced
1 large avocado, peeled, pitted, and diced
1/4 cup pimiento-stuffed olives, halved crosswise
2 tablespoons finely chopped coriander or parsley
1/4 teaspoon crushed dried oregano (optional)
Lettuce leaves
3 canned jalapeño chilies, seeded and cut into strips

Combine the shrimp and onion in a bowl. Beat together the oil, lemon juice, and salt and pepper with a fork or whisk until well blended and pour over the shrimp and onion. Allow to marinate 3 to 4 hours in the refrigerator, stirring several times. Just before serving, add the tomato, avocado, olives, coriander, and oregano. Toss gently but thoroughly. Serve on the lettuce leaves, garnished with the jalapeño chilies.

SHRIMP SALAD WITH PINEAPPLE

The pineapple contributes a delightful shock of unexpected piquancy.

Serves 6
2 pounds cooked large shrimp, shelled and cut in half lengthwise
1-1/2 cups Fruit French Dressing, page 139, or Curry Fruit French Dressing, page 140
5 cups diced fresh pineapple
2 medium tomatoes, quartered, seeded, and diced
2 medium avocados, peeled, pitted, and diced
Lettuce leaves

In a large bowl combine the shrimp with the dressing. Cover and refrigerate 30 minutes, stirring twice. Add the pineapple, tomatoes, and avocados and toss gently but thoroughly. Taste and adjust the seasoning. Serve in a bowl lined with the lettuce leaves.

Note You may serve this salad in pineapple shells. Prepare 3 small ripe pineapples as described in the recipe for Pineapple on the Half Shell, page 123. Combine the cubed pineapple meat with the shrimp, tomatoes, and avocados and heap into the pineapple shells. Garnish the salad with mint sprigs if desired.

THAI SHRIMP SALAD

Exotic and tantalizing.

Serves 4 to 6
2 quarts water
1 bay leaf
1 tablespoon salt
1 teaspoon black peppercorns
2 pounds medium shrimp
2 tablespoons peanut or olive oil
1/3 cup finely chopped shallots or
　　scallions
1 large clove garlic, finely chopped
1 cup finely chopped green or sweet
　　red pepper
1 medium tart apple, peeled, cored,
　　and finely chopped
1/3 cup chopped peanuts
2 tablespoons soy sauce
1/2 cup or more coconut milk, follow-
　　ing (or substitute canned coconut
　　milk)
Salt to taste
Romaine lettuce leaves, shredded
Lime wedges

Bring the water, bay leaf, salt, and peppercorns to a boil over high heat. Add the shrimp and cook 5 minutes or until tender. Drain and cool. Shell and devein the shrimp and cut in half. Set the shrimp aside.

In a small, heavy skillet heat the oil over moderate heat. Add the shallots and garlic and sauté until soft but not browned, stirring frequently. Remove from the heat. Transfer the contents of the skillet into a bowl and allow to cool to room temperature. Add the green pepper, apple, peanuts, soy sauce, and coconut milk and mix well. Add the shrimp and toss gently but thoroughly. Taste and add salt if necessary. Cover and chill 1 hour. Serve on the shredded lettuce, accompanied by the lime wedges.

Note One mango, peeled, seeded, and cut into thin strips, may be substituted for the apple. The shrimp may be broiled rather than boiled. Instead of the chopped pepper, you may hold 2 peppers on a long-handled fork over a flame, turning slowly until the skins are charred. Peel off the skins and slice the peppers into thin strips, discarding the seeds.

Coconut Milk Combine 1/2 cup diced coconut meat with 1/2 cup hot water in the container of an electric blender. Blend until the coconut is very finely grated, almost puréed, then squeeze through a double thickness of dampened cheesecloth to extract all the liquid. If you have no blender, soak 1/2 cup freshly grated coconut meat in 1/2 cup hot water 30 minutes, then squeeze through cheesecloth as above.

Meat, Poultry, and Seafood Salads

LOBSTER SALAD

Serves 6

1 pound cooked lobster meat, cut
  into 1-inch pieces
Lemon French Dressing, page 138, or
  Italian Dressing, page 143
Lettuce leaves
Lobster claws
3 hard-cooked eggs, cut into wedges
Pitted black olives
Mayonnaise, page 146 (optional)

In a bowl toss the lobster meat with
the dressing gently but thoroughly.
Cover and refrigerate 1 hour, stirring
occasionally. Line a serving platter
with the lettuce leaves. Pile the lobster
meat on the lettuce. Garnish with the
lobster claws, eggs, and olives. Serve as
is or with the mayonnaise.

Caribbean Lobster Salad Variation
Marinate the lobster meat in the dressing as above, then combine with 2
cups diced fresh pineapple. Garnish
with avocado slices, pitted black
olives, and lime wedges. Serve with
Curry-Lemon French Dressing, page
138, or Curry Mayonnaise, page 148.
Or combine 1 cup Mayonnaise, page
146, or sour cream (or 1/2 cup of
each), and the grated rind and juice of
1 lime until well blended.

SOUTH PACIFIC LOBSTER SALAD

Serves 4

8 ounces diced cooked lobster meat
1 cup diced papaya
1 cup diced mango
1 cup thinly sliced celery
1/4 cup heavy cream
1 teaspoon coconut milk, page 103
  (optional)
2 teaspoons freshly squeezed and
  strained lime juice
1/4 teaspoon grated lime rind
1 teaspoon grated onion
1/4 teaspoon freshly grated ginger
1 teaspoon soy sauce
Salt and freshly ground black pepper
  to taste
Romaine lettuce leaves
Watercress
2 tablespoons toasted chopped
  macadamia nuts or slivered almonds

Combine the lobster, papaya, mango,
and celery in a bowl. Mix together the
cream, coconut milk, lime juice, lime
rind, onion, ginger, soy sauce, and salt
and pepper. Pour over the salad and
toss gently but thoroughly. Taste and
adjust the seasoning. Serve on the lettuce leaves, garnished with the watercress and macadamia nuts.

SPANISH SEAFOOD SALAD

Serves 4

8 ounces cooked shrimp, shelled,
  deveined, and coarsely chopped
8 ounces cooked lobster meat,
  coarsely chopped
8 ounces cooked crab meat, coarsely
  chopped
2 hard-cooked eggs, coarsely chopped
1 small mild onion, finely chopped
1/4 cup finely chopped green pepper
1/4 cup pitted black olives (preferably
  Greek olives)
1/4 cup pimiento-stuffed olives,
  sliced
1 tablespoon capers
1/4 cup olive oil
2 tablespoons wine vinegar
1 tablespoon freshly squeezed and
  strained lemon juice
1 tablespoon finely chopped chives
1/8 teaspoon crushed dried thyme
Salt and freshly ground black pepper
  to taste
Lettuce leaves

Combine the shrimp, lobster, crab,
eggs, onion, green pepper, black olives,
green olives, and capers in a mixing
bowl. Beat together the oil, vinegar,
lemon juice, chives, thyme, and salt
and pepper with a fork or whisk until
well blended and pour over the salad.
Toss gently but thoroughly. Cover and
chill. Serve on the lettuce leaves.

STUFFED AVOCADO SALAD PLATE

A handsome way to serve avocado, which has a decided affinity with shrimp, crab, or lobster.

Serves 6

12 ounces cooked medium shrimp or
    lobster meat, diced
3 hard-cooked eggs, coarsely chopped
3 scallions, finely chopped, including
    2 inches of the green tops
1/2 cup finely chopped celery heart
1-1/2 cups Herb French Dressing,
    page 138, or Herb Mayonnaise,
    page 148
3 large avocados
Juice of 1 lemon, freshly squeezed
    and strained
Boston or leaf lettuce leaves
French Potato Salad, page 67
    (optional)
2 medium ripe tomatoes, sliced
1 medium green pepper, seeded, de-
    ribbed, and sliced in rings
Pitted black olives

In a small bowl combine the shrimp, eggs, scallions, celery, and 3/4 cup of the dressing. Toss gently but thoroughly. Cover and refrigerate 2 hours or until chilled. Close to serving time, halve the unpeeled avocados lengthwise. Remove the pits. Brush with the lemon juice to prevent discoloration. Place each avocado half on an individual salad plate lined with lettuce leaves and fill with the shrimp mixture. Decorate each serving with a small mound of the potato salad, tomato slices, green pepper rings, and olives. Pass the remaining 3/4 cup dressing in a cruet.

STUFFED TOMATO
SALAD PLATE

Try this rather elegant but easy recipe when you have flavorful, ripe, and firm tomatoes.

Serves 6

6 medium firm tomatoes, peeled
2 cups fresh cooked crab meat, or
    2 7-ounce cans crab meat, rinsed
    and drained
1 tablespoon freshly squeezed and
    strained lemon juice
1/4 cup finely chopped mild onion
1/3 cup finely chopped celery
2 tablespoons finely chopped parsley
1/3 cup Mayonnaise, page 146
Salt and freshly ground black pepper
    to taste
Romaine or Boston lettuce leaves
1 6-ounce jar marinated artichokes,
    drained
1 avocado, peeled, pitted, and sliced
1 medium cucumber, peeled and sliced
3 hard-cooked eggs, quartered
12 pitted black olives
12 pimiento-stuffed olives
Additional mayonnaise for dressing
    (optional)

With the stem ends pointing down, cut each tomato into 6 slices, cutting to, but not through, the bases. Spread the slices apart slightly. Combine the crab, lemon juice, onion, celery, parsley, 1/3 cup mayonnaise, and salt and pepper and mix well. Taste and adjust the seasoning. Sprinkle the cut surfaces of the tomatoes with salt. Fill in between the slices with the crab mixture. Arrange the filled tomatoes on individual plates lined with the lettuce leaves. Garnish with the artichoke hearts, avocado, cucumber, eggs, and olives. Serve with additional mayonnaise if you like.

STUFFED ARTICHOKE SALAD PLATE

Serves 6

6 large artichokes
Juice of 1 lemon, freshly squeezed
    and strained
2 cups French Dressing, page 138
1-1/2 pounds cooked shrimp or crab
    meat, or a combination
Lettuce leaves
3 hard-cooked eggs, sliced
1 16-ounce jar pickled beets, well
    drained and sliced
1 small cucumber, sliced
Pitted black olives
1 cup Herb Mayonnaise, page 148, or
    additional French dressing

Prepare each artichoke as follows: Remove any coarse outer leaves and cut 1 inch off the tops of the remaining leaves. Separate the top leaves and pull out the thorny pinkish leaves from the center. With a spoon scrape out the fuzzy choke underneath, being careful not to puncture the meaty part. Cut off the stem and drop the artichoke into a bowl of salted water mixed with the lemon juice (this prevents discoloration).

Drain the artichokes and cook them in boiling salted water about 40 minutes or until tender. With a perforated spoon lift the artichokes from the water and place them upside down on paper towels to drain.

In a large bowl combine the drained artichokes with 1 cup of the dressing. Cover and refrigerate until chilled, spooning the dressing over them several times. In another bowl combine the shrimp with the remaining 1 cup dressing. Cover and marinate in the refrigerator until chilled, stirring several times.

To serve, remove each artichoke from the dressing and place it on an individual salad plate lined with lettuce leaves. Fill the center with the marinated shrimp. Garnish with the sliced eggs, beets, and cucumber and the olives. Serve with the mayonnaise.

Note Curry Mayonnaise, page 148, may be substituted for the herb mayonnaise.

ITALIAN MIXED SALAD WITH TUNA

Serves 4

2 medium cloves garlic, halved
4 large tomatoes, peeled, seeded, and
    cut into wedges
1 medium green pepper, seeded,
    deribbed, and thinly sliced
1 medium cucumber, peeled and
    thinly sliced
1 very small mild onion, finely sliced
Finely chopped basil to taste
2 anchovy fillets, finely chopped
1/4 teaspoon crushed dried oregano
8 pitted black olives (preferably
    Mediterranean olives)
2 hard-cooked eggs, cut into wedges
Salt and freshly ground black pepper
    to taste
1 8-ounce can tuna, flaked (preferably
    Italian *ventresca* tuna)
Olive oil to taste

Rub a salad bowl thoroughly with the pieces of garlic. Arrange all the ingredients except the oil in the bowl in the order given, distributing the garlic pieces here and there. Sprinkle with the oil, stir gently, and let stand 1 hour. Remove the garlic pieces. Stir the salad again, taste and adjust the seasoning, and serve.

TARAMASALATA

A well-known Greek delicacy also favored by Armenians.

Serves 6
3 slices white bread, trimmed of crusts
1/4 cup *tarama* (salted carp roe) or
    red caviar
2 tablespoons freshly squeezed and
    strained lemon juice
2 tablespoons grated onion, or
    1 small clove garlic, crushed
1/3 to 1/2 cup olive oil
Lettuce leaves
Black olives (preferably Greek olives)
Thin toast or crackers (optional)

Dip the bread in water and squeeze dry. Place it and the *tarama* in the container of an electric blender and blend until smooth. Keeping the motor running, remove the cover and add the lemon juice, onion, and enough of the oil in a slow, steady stream to make a thick, creamy mixture. (Alternately, place the soaked bread, squeezed dry, in a shallow bowl. Add the *tarama* a little at a time, mashing and mixing it with a spoon. Beat in the lemon juice, onion, and enough of the oil, a tablespoon at a time, to make a thick, creamy mixture.) Taste and adjust the seasoning. Cover and chill. Serve over the lettuce leaves, garnished with the olives and accompanied with thin toast or crackers, if desired.

FUJIYAMA SALAD

Serves 4
2 pounds mussels in their shells
1 small onion
1 small carrot
1 stalk celery
1/2 cup dry white wine
3 medium potatoes, boiled in jackets
2 hard-cooked eggs, chopped
1/2 cup French Dressing, page 138
1 tablespoon finely chopped parsley
1 tablespoon finely chopped chives
1 tablespoon finely chopped mild
    onion
2 hard-cooked egg whites, finely
    chopped
Green pepper rings
Parsley sprigs

Scrub the mussel shells with a stiff brush or stainless steel scouring pad under cold running water. In a heavy saucepan combine the mussels with the onion, carrot, celery, and wine. Cook over high heat until the shells open. Drain, reserving the cooking liquid. When cool enough to handle, remove the mussels from their shells. Discard any that do not open. Set the mussels aside.

Peel and slice the potatoes while hot. Sprinkle with 1/4 cup of the reserved liquid from the mussels. Combine the potatoes, mussels, and eggs in a mixing bowl. Mix together the French dressing, parsley, chives, and onion and pour over the salad. Toss gently but thoroughly. Taste and adjust the seasoning.

Shape the mixture into a cone on a platter. Cover and chill. Just before serving cover the peak with the egg whites to simulate snow. Garnish with the green pepper and parsley sprigs.

Note Truffles may be added to this salad and oysters or clams may be substituted for the mussels.

HERRING SALAD

Serves 6

1 8-ounce jar pickled herring in
    wine sauce
4 medium potatoes, cooked, peeled,
    and cubed
2 large tart green apples, peeled,
    cored, and chopped
1-1/2 cups peeled and diced cooked
    beets
4 dill pickles, chopped
1 small mild red or white onion,
    finely chopped
2 tablespoons finely chopped parsley
3/4 cup olive oil
3 hard-cooked egg yolks
1 teaspoon salt
1/4 teaspoon freshly ground black
    pepper or to taste
3 tablespoons wine vinegar
Bibb or Boston lettuce leaves
Sliced and drained pickled beets

In a large bowl combine the herring, potatoes, apples, cooked beets, pickles, onion, and parsley. Add 2 tablespoons of the oil and toss lightly. In a small bowl mash the egg yolks with a fork. Season with the salt and pepper. Gradually beat in the remaining oil, then the vinegar until the mixture is well blended and smooth. Gently bind the salad with this dressing. Line a serving platter with the lettuce leaves. Arrange the salad in a mound over them and garnish with the pickled beet slices. Serve chilled.

Variation Substitute 1/2 cup French Dressing, page 138, for the above dressing. Add 2 hard-cooked eggs, chopped, with the herring. If desired, serve the salad with additional dressing or Mayonnaise, page 146.

ANTIPASTO SALAD PLATE

Line a large platter or tray with a bed of romaine or Boston lettuce leaves. Top with an array of foods chosen from those suggested below, using contrasting colors, textures, and flavors. The finished platter should include meat, fish, raw and cooked vegetables, olives, and eggs. Serve olive oil and wine vinegar separately.

Canned tuna, drained and broken
    into chunks
Sardines in oil, drained
Anchovy fillets, rolled or flat, drained
Italian salami, thinly sliced
Prosciutto, very thinly sliced and
    rolled up
Mortadella, thinly sliced and rolled up
Provolone, Bel Paese, or Fontina
    cheese, sliced
Marinated artichokes or Artichokes
    Vinaigrette, page 53, drained
Pickled mushrooms, drained and
    sliced
Italian pickled vegetables, drained and
    sliced
Pickled beets, drained and sliced
Peperoncini (bottled hot Italian
    peppers), drained
Small cherry tomatoes, or medium
    tomatoes cut into wedges
Radish slices or rosettes
Green pepper rings or slices
Pimiento strips
Scallions, trimmed
Fennel or celery hearts, cut into strips
Cucumbers, peeled if necessary and
    thinly sliced
Italian Red Bean or Chick-Pea Salad,
    page 56, served in Boston lettuce
    cups
Black or green olives
Hard-cooked eggs, quartered or sliced

Fruit Salads

Some of the world's most fascinating salads feature fruit as an essential ingredient. Especially popular among them are those served as dessert, and purists may look down upon fruit salads except for dessert. Nevertheless, fruits play an equally important role in the creation of many exciting and original salads that can open a meal, accompany a meal, or even be the meal itself (see other chapters in this book).

Fruit salads can be sweet, tart, or both. As a general rule it is advisable to choose a fairly tart dressing for pre-dessert fruit salads in order to avoid dulling the appetite. Dessert salads, on the other hand, can have either a light and piquant dressing or one that is opulent and sweet.

The lovely shapes and colors of fruits can lend beauty and a sunny mood to any menu. A lavish display of attractively arranged sliced fruit, presented if you wish with a choice of complementary dressings, makes an impressive addition to a buffet table or can even substitute for flowers as a centerpiece.

To prevent fruits such as bananas, peaches, and apples from darkening after cutting, brush them with lemon juice.

FRUIT SALAD WITH OLIVES

Serves 4

2 cups grapefruit sections (remove
    the seeds and white membrane)
1 cup orange sections (remove the
    seeds and white membrane)
2 cups cubed fresh pineapple
1/2 cup pitted black olives, sliced
Fruit French Dressing, page 139

Combine the grapefruit, orange, pineapple, and olives in a serving bowl.
Cover and chill. Just before serving
add the dressing and toss gently but
thoroughly.

PAPAYA, ORANGE, AND AVOCADO SALAD

A lively, exotic temptation.

Serves 4

1 papaya, peeled, seeded, and sliced
2 oranges, peeled, seeded, and sec-
    tioned (remove the white
    membrane)
2 ripe avocados, peeled, pitted, and
    sliced
6 tablespoons olive oil
6 tablespoons freshly squeezed and
    strained lemon juice
2 scallions, finely chopped, including
    2 inches of the green tops
1/2 to 3/4 teaspoon chili powder
Salt and freshly ground black pepper
    to taste

Combine the papaya, oranges, and avocados in a salad bowl. Beat together
the remaining ingredients with a fork
or whisk until well blended and pour
over the fruit. Cover and refrigerate
several hours, turning the fruit 2 or 3
times. Serve chilled.

PAPAYA AND PINEAPPLE DELIGHT

Here is a superbly refreshing way to
begin or end a meal.

Serves 4

2 cups diced ripe papaya
2 cups diced fresh pineapple
1/4 cup superfine sugar or to taste
1/4 cup freshly squeezed and strained
    lime juice
Mint sprigs (optional)

Combine the papaya and pineapple in
a bowl. Sprinkle with the sugar and
lime juice. Toss gently but thoroughly.
Cover and chill. Serve garnished with
the mint sprigs if you like.

Note Serve this salad in individual
sherbet glasses or in papaya halves.
(Cut 2 papayas in half lengthwise. Remove and discard the seeds.)

TROPICAL FRUIT SALAD

Serves 6

1 cup diced honeydew melon
1 cup diced cantaloupe
1 cup diced apples
1 cup sliced fresh peaches
1 cup strawberries, hulled
1 cup seedless grapes
1 cup diced Gruyère or Swiss cheese
1 cup finely chopped pitted dates
1 cup finely chopped walnuts or pecans
Honey-Lime Dressing I, page 152
2 medium bananas
2 tablespoons freshly squeezed and
    strained lime or lemon juice
    mixed with a little water
Romaine or leaf lettuce leaves
Strawberries, hulled

Combine the honeydew, cantaloupe, apples, peaches, strawberries, grapes, cheese, dates, and 1/2 cup of the walnuts. Add the dressing and toss lightly but thoroughly. Set aside.

Peel the bananas. Cut each one diagonally crosswise into 3 equal pieces, then halve the pieces lengthwise. Dip the bananas in the lime-water mixture, then roll each piece in the remaining 1/2 cup walnuts.

To serve, mound the salad in a bowl lined with the lettuce. Garnish with the nut-covered banana pieces and strawberries.

HAWAIIAN FRUIT SALAD

Serves 6

1 cup cubed fresh pineapple
1 cup orange sections (remove the
    seeds and white membrane)
1 cup cubed papaya
1 cup cubed mango
1 cup strawberry halves
1 cup seedless grapes
1 cup banana slices
1/2 cup freshly grated coconut
Sour Cream, Honey, and
    Crème de Menthe Dressing, page
    159
Whole strawberries, hulled
Mint sprigs

Combine the pineapple, orange, papaya, mango, strawberry halves, grapes, banana slices, and coconut in a bowl. Add the dressing and mix lightly but thoroughly. Cover and chill. Serve garnished with the whole strawberries and mint sprigs.

SOUTH PACIFIC FRUIT COMPOTE

Serves 6 to 8
2 cups cubed fresh pineapple
1 cup cubed papaya
1 cup cubed guava
1 cup cubed sweet apple
1 cup pitted cherries
1 cup medium strawberries, hulled
1 cup banana slices
1 cup orange sections (remove the seeds and white membrane)
1/4 cup toasted macadamia nuts, halved
1/2 cup Cognac
1/2 cup Cointreau or Triple Sec
2 tablespoons sugar
Mint sprigs

Combine the pineapple, papaya, guava, apple, cherries, strawberries, banana, orange, and macadamia nuts in a bowl. Mix together the Cognac and Cointreau with the sugar and pour over the salad. Cover and chill 1 hour. Serve in individual glass compotes garnished with the mint sprigs.

KOREAN FRUIT BOWL

Serves 4
1 cup freshly squeezed and strained orange juice
1 cup water
1/2 cup sugar
1/2 teaspoon ground cinnamon
1 large orange, peeled, seeded, and sectioned (remove the white membrane)
1 cup strawberries, hulled and sliced
1 large banana, peeled and sliced
2 tablespoons chopped blanched almonds or pine nuts

In a small saucepan combine the orange juice, water, sugar, and cinnamon. Bring to a boil over high heat, stirring constantly to dissolve the sugar. Reduce the heat and simmer until a syrup is formed. Remove from the heat and cool. Combine the orange, strawberries, and banana in a bowl. Pour the syrup over the fruit. Cover and chill. Serve sprinkled with the almonds.

Note Other fruits such as pears, peaches, or cherries can be used.

WEST AFRICAN FRUIT SALAD

Serves 6
1 cup sugar
2 cups water
1 teaspoon freshly squeezed and strained lemon juice
Thinly peeled rind of 1 orange
1 cup diced fresh pineapple
1 cup diced papaya
1 cup orange sections (remove seeds and white membrane)
1 cup diced peaches
1/2 cup pitted and halved cherries
2 bananas, peeled and sliced
1/2 cup chopped roasted peanuts or freshly grated coconut

In a small saucepan combine the sugar, water, lemon juice, and orange rind. Bring to a boil over high heat, stirring constantly to dissolve the sugar. Reduce the heat and simmer until a syrup is formed. Remove from the heat and cool. Remove the orange rind and discard. Combine the pineapple, papaya, orange, peaches, cherries, and bananas in a serving bowl. Pour the syrup over the fruit and stir gently. Cover and chill. Serve sprinkled with the peanuts.

LEBANESE FRESH FRUIT SALAD

Serves 4

1 cup sugar
2 cups water
1 large apple, peeled, cored, and
   sliced in rings
1 cup diced fresh pineapple
2 bananas, peeled and sliced
2 tablespoons seedless golden raisins
2 tablespoons pine nuts
1 cup strawberries, hulled and halved
1/2 teaspoon orange flower water
1/2 teaspoon rose water

In a small saucepan combine the sugar and water. Bring to a boil over high heat, stirring constantly to dissolve the sugar. Reduce the heat and simmer 10 to 15 minutes or until syrupy. Remove from the heat and add the apple, pineapple, bananas, raisins, and pine nuts. Allow to cool to room temperature, then transfer the contents of the saucepan into a serving bowl. Cover and refrigerate until thoroughly chilled. Stir in the strawberries, sprinkle with the orange flower water and rose water, and serve.

NORTH AFRICAN ORANGE AND OLIVE SALAD

Serves 4

3 medium oranges, peeled, seeded,
   and diced (remove the white
   membrane)
1 17-ounce can pitted black olives,
   drained
Pinch ground cumin
Salt and cayenne pepper to taste
Freshly squeezed and strained lemon
   juice to taste

Combine the oranges and olives in a serving bowl. Sprinkle with the cumin, salt and cayenne pepper, and lemon juice. Toss gently but thoroughly. Taste and adjust the seasoning. Cover and chill 1 hour before serving.

MIDDLE EAST DRIED FRUIT SALAD

Delicately contrived and exotically perfumed.

Serves 4

1 cup dried apricots
1/2 cup dried prunes
1/2 cup seedless golden raisins
1 tablespoon pomegranate seeds
   (optional)
1/4 cup whole blanched almonds
2 tablespoons shelled unsalted
   pistachios
2 tablespoons pine nuts
1/4 cup sugar or to taste
1 teaspoon orange flower water
1 teaspoon rose water

Combine the apricots, prunes, raisins, pomegranate seeds, almonds, pistachios, and pine nuts in a bowl. Cover with water, stir in the sugar, and add the orange flower water and rose water. Allow the fruit to soak at room temperature 48 hours. Chill thoroughly before serving.

Fruit Salads

FRUIT SALAD SCHEHERAZADE

A harmonious Iraqi combination of fresh and dried fruits moistened with orange juice and speckled with chopped toasted almonds.

Serves 4

2 large oranges, peeled, seeded, and diced (remove the white membrane)
1 medium apple, peeled, cored, and diced
2 bananas, peeled and diced
1/3 cup chopped pitted dates
2 tablespoons finely chopped dried figs
1 tablespoon sugar or to taste
1 cup freshly squeezed and strained orange juice
1/4 cup chopped toasted blanched almonds
2 tablespoons freshly grated coconut (optional)

Combine the oranges, apple, bananas, dates, and figs in a serving bowl. Dissolve the sugar in the orange juice and pour over the fruit. Cover and chill thoroughly. Serve sprinkled with the almonds and coconut.

PEAR AND CHEESE SALAD

Very Italian, and very elegant.

Serves 4
4 medium winter pears, peeled, cored,
    and chopped
4 ounces Gruyère or Emmenthal
    cheese, cut in julienne
1/4 cup chopped walnuts (preferably
    freshly shelled)
1/2 cup Lemon French Dressing,
    page 138

Combine the pears, cheese, and walnuts in a salad bowl. Add the dressing and toss gently but thoroughly. Taste and adjust the seasoning and serve.

DIETER'S FRUIT PLATTER

When I worked as a fashion model in New York City, the following luncheon salad, minus the shredded coconut and mint, provided a faithful summer standby for me and other models who required good nourishment but could not afford too many calories.

Serves 4
1/2 large cantaloupe (halved cross-
    wise), seeded
Lettuce leaves
2 cups low-fat cottage cheese, drained
2 cups strawberries or raspberries,
    dipped in superfine sugar if desired
2 cups watermelon balls
2 medium oranges, peeled and sliced
    (remove the seeds and white
    membrane)
2 medium bananas
2 tablespoons freshly squeezed and
    strained lime or lemon juice
    mixed with a little water
1/2 cup freshly shredded coconut
    (optional)
Mint sprigs (optional)

Slice the cantaloupe into 4 wedges like a cake. Place it in the middle of a serving platter lined with the lettuce leaves and fill the hollow center with the cottage cheese. Arrange the strawberries, watermelon balls, and orange slices attractively around the cantaloupe. Peel the bananas. Cut them diagonally crosswise into 4 equal pieces, then halve the pieces lengthwise. Dip the bananas in the lime-water mixture, then roll each piece in the shredded coconut. Garnish the platter with the coconut-covered banana pieces and mint sprigs and serve.

Note Other fresh fruits in season, such as pineapple, grapes, blueberries, peaches, pears, or apricots may be substituted for those suggested above.

BUFFET FRUIT PLATTER

Select an assortment of your favorite fruits, or choose some from the following: pineapple, strawberries or raspberries, peaches or nectarines, pears, honeydew, cantaloupe, bananas, papaya, oranges, grapefruits, cherries, green grapes, and pomegranates. Allow about 1 cup fruit for each serving. Peel, pare, seed, and core the fruit as necessary. Cut large fruit into bite-size portions and arrange in a decorative pattern on a large tray. (To prevent peaches, pears, and bananas from darkening, brush them with lemon juice.) Serve accompanied with bowls of lemon or lime slices, sugar, freshly grated coconut, and Sour Cream and Strawberry Dressing, page 158, or Sour Cream and Honey Dressing, page 159. Allow each person to make his own selection.

PINEAPPLE ON THE HALF SHELL

Serves 6

Cut 1 large pineapple in half lengthwise, including the leaves. Carefully scoop out the meat and discard the core. Freeze the pineapple shells 2 hours. Meanwhile, cube the pineapple meat and combine in a bowl with hulled and halved strawberries and, if desired, other cut-up fruits such as papaya, guava, orange, mango, and banana. Sprinkle with rum and superfine sugar to taste. Toss gently, cover, and chill. To serve, spoon the fruit into the pineapple shells. Sprinkle with additional rum if you like and garnish with mint sprigs.

WATERMELON BOWL

Serves 6

Choose a well-shaped watermelon for this dish. Cut it in half and reserve one half for another use. With a melon ball cutter remove the pulp. Discard the seeds. Combine the melon balls with any desired fruit such as cantaloupe and honeydew melon balls, pineapple chunks, seedless grapes, and blueberries. Pour 1/2 cup or more sweet sherry or port over the fruit and toss lightly. Heap into the watermelon shell and chill.

Variation Omit the sherry or port. Combine the watermelon balls with cut-up pineapple, papaya, banana, orange, and grapefruit. Sprinkle with 1 cup freshly shredded coconut and 1/2 cup sugar or to taste. Toss lightly. Heap into the watermelon shell and chill before serving.

Molded Salads

On a hot summer evening what could be lovelier than a brilliantly clear, shimmering aspic, elegant enough to climax a buffet or outdoor party? And mousses, although they don't glisten, are equally enticing.

Molded salads may require a little effort, but they can be prepared well in advance of serving time, and even the simplest of them has a festive air about it. Food often looks more dramatic when presented in molded form, and this is an ingenious way to transform leftovers or everyday ingredients.

The addition of wine lends distinction to many molded salads and heightens their flavor. Dry white wine or dry sherry goes well with savory salads, while sweeter wines, such as sauterne, or fruit-flavored liqueurs are good with fruit.

Molds come in an assortment of fanciful designs and shapes. The choice of mold depends on the dish and your personal preference. A seafood aspic, for instance, is very effective when made in a fish-shaped mold. Rather than using a large mold, you might occasionally choose individual decorative ones.

Molded salads bring variety to a menu and may be served as appetizers, side dishes, or desserts, and, with the addition of meat, poultry, or fish, they can become luncheon or supper main courses.

Here are some hints on the molding and unmolding of gelatin salads: Before molding your salad, be sure to taste it and adjust the seasoning. Do not use more gelatin than the amount specified in a recipe; otherwise the salad will have a rubbery texture and unpleasant taste. Always use the exact size mold called for and fill it to the top. A jellied mixture is more easily removed when a mold has been moistened with cold water and chilled before filling. Refrigerate the salad thoroughly, preferably overnight. To unmold it, have ready a chilled serving platter large enough to allow for a garnish. Run the pointed tip of a knife around the edges of the mold to release the vacuum that holds the salad to it. Dip the mold up to the rim into a basin of hot water for just a few seconds. Place the serving platter upside down over the mold. Hold the platter and mold together and invert. Shake gently to release the gelatin. If it does not release, re-dip the mold quickly into hot water, or briefly cover the inverted mold with a hot, damp cloth. Shake again to release. Carefully lift off the mold. Garnish the platter as desired and refrigerate until ready to serve.

Molded Salads

ROQUEFORT MOLD

A handsome cold dish for a buffet table.

Serves 6
4 ounces Roquefort cheese
1/2 cup sour cream
2 tablespoons freshly squeezed and
    strained lemon juice
1/4 teaspoon garlic salt
1/4 teaspoon salt
1 envelope (1 tablespoon) unflavored
    gelatin
1/4 cup cold water
1 cup heavy cream, whipped
1 pound cooked small shrimp,
    marinated in Lemon French
    Dressing, page 138
1 medium cucumber, thinly sliced
12 cherry tomatoes
Watercress

Mash the cheese. Add the sour cream, lemon juice, garlic salt, and salt and blend thoroughly. Soften the gelatin in the cold water and dissolve over hot water. Gradually add the dissolved gelatin to the cheese mixture and beat until smooth. Fold in the whipped cream. Taste and adjust the seasoning. Turn into a rinsed and chilled 1-quart mold. Cover with foil and chill thoroughly until firm. To serve, unmold on a platter and decorate with the shrimp, cucumber, tomatoes, and watercress.

AVOCADO MOLD

Serves 6
3 large avocados, peeled, pitted,
    and mashed
1/3 cup freshly squeezed and
    strained lime juice
2 tablespoons finely chopped water-
    cress
1 tablespoon finely chopped chives or
    scallions (optional)
3/4 teaspoon salt or to taste
6 ounces cream cheese, at room
    temperature
1 cup milk or light cream
1 envelope (1 tablespoon) unflavored
    gelatin
1/4 cup cold water
1 pound cooked small shrimp
Lime French Dressing, page 139
Lime slices
Watercress

Combine the avocados, lime juice, chopped watercress, chives, and salt. Mash the cheese. Gradually add the avocado mixture and the milk and blend thoroughly. Soften the gelatin in the cold water and dissolve it over hot water. Add the dissolved gelatin to the avocado mixture and blend well. Taste and adjust the seasoning. Turn into a rinsed and chilled 6-cup mold. Cover with foil and chill until set. Combine the shrimp with the dressing, cover, and chill.

To serve, unmold the avocado salad on a platter. Decorate with the shrimp, lime slices, and watercress.

Variation Prepare the salad in a ring mold. Unmold on a platter lined with greens and fill the center with a crab or lobster salad. Omit the shrimp.

TOMATO ASPIC

Serves 4

2 envelopes (2 tablespoons) unflavored gelatin
1/2 cup cold water
1/2 cup rich beef broth, heated
2 cups tomato juice
2 tablespoons tomato paste (optional)
2 tablespoons freshly squeezed and strained lemon juice
1 tablespoon grated onion
1 tablespoon finely chopped parsley
1 teaspoon crushed dried tarragon
1/4 teaspoon Worcestershire sauce
3/4 teaspoon salt
1/8 teaspoon Tabasco sauce
1 avocado, peeled, pitted, and diced, or 2 hard-cooked eggs, chopped
1/4 cup chopped celery or cucumber
1 pound cooked small shrimp, marinated in Lemon French Dressing, page 138
Chicory leaves (or other salad greens)

In a large bowl soften the gelatin in the water. Add the beef broth, stirring until the gelatin dissolves. Add the tomato juice, tomato paste, lemon juice, onion, parsley, tarragon, Worcestershire sauce, salt, and Tabasco sauce. Cover and refrigerate until partially set. Carefully fold in the avocado and celery. Taste and adjust the seasoning. Turn into a rinsed and chilled 1-quart ring mold. Cover with foil and refrigerate until set.

To serve, unmold on a platter and fill the center of the ring with the shrimp. Surround with the chicory.

Molded Salads

SALMON MOUSSE

Serves 6

1 envelope (1 tablespoon) unflavored
    gelatin
1/4 cup cold water
1/2 cup boiling water
1/2 cup Mayonnaise, page 146
1 tablespoon grated onion
1 tablespoon freshly squeezed and
    strained lemon juice
1/4 teaspoon Tabasco sauce
1/4 teaspoon paprika
3/4 teaspoon salt or to taste
1 16-ounce can salmon, drained,
    picked over, and finely chopped
1 tablespoon finely chopped dill
1/2 cup heavy cream, whipped
Watercress
Sour Cream and Dill Dressing, page 157

Soften the gelatin in the cold water. Add the boiling water and stir to dissolve the gelatin. Add the mayonnaise, onion, lemon juice, Tabasco sauce, paprika, and salt and mix well. Cover and chill until partially set. Add the salmon and dill and beat until thoroughly blended. Fold in the whipped cream. Taste and adjust the seasoning. Turn into a rinsed and chilled 6-cup ring mold. Cover with foil and chill until set.

Unmold on a platter and fill the center with the watercress. Serve with the sour cream and dill dressing.

TUNA MOUSSE

This delicious mousse can highlight a summer luncheon.

Serves 4 to 6

2 7-ounce cans tuna, drained thoroughly and ground
2 tablespoons finely chopped onion
1/2 cup Mayonnaise, page 146, or
    Herb Mayonnaise, page 148
2 tablespoons freshly squeezed and
    strained lemon juice
1 envelope (1 tablespoon) unflavored
    gelatin
1/4 cup cold water
1 cup sour cream
2 tablespoons finely chopped parsley
    or pimiento-stuffed olives
Salt to taste
Lettuce leaves or watercress
Cherry tomatoes
Cucumber slices
Sliced hard-cooked eggs

Combine the tuna, onion, mayonnaise, and lemon juice in a bowl. Beat until smooth. Soften the gelatin in the cold water and dissolve over hot water. Add the dissolved gelatin, sour cream, parsley, and salt to the tuna mixture. Blend thoroughly. Taste and adjust the seasoning. Turn into a rinsed and chilled 3-1/2-cup mold. Cover with foil and chill thoroughly until firm. To serve, unmold on a platter lined with the lettuce and garnish with the tomatoes, cucumber slices, and hard-cooked egg slices.

VEGETABLE AND SHELLFISH MOLD

Serves 6

2 cups chicken or fish broth
2 envelopes (2 tablespoons) unflav-
    ored gelatin
1/4 cup peeled and diced cooked
    potatoes
1/4 cup diced cooked carrots
1/4 cup diced cooked green beans or
    peas
1/4 cup finely chopped parsley
1 tablespoon finely chopped chives
1 tablespoon finely chopped basil,
    tarragon, or dill (optional)
1/2 cup French Dressing, page 138
Salt and freshly ground black pepper
    to taste
1/4 cup cold water
2 cups Mayonnaise, page 146
1/2 cup diced cooked lobster or
    crab meat
Watercress sprigs

In a saucepan heat 1-3/4 cups of the broth. Soften 1 envelope of the gelatin in the remaining 1/4 cup cold broth. Stir into the hot broth until dissolved. Cool. Coat a 6-cup mold with 1/2 cup of the cooled aspic. Chill; repeat 3 times. (Reserve the remaining aspic for other uses.)

Combine the potatoes, carrots, green beans, parsley, chives, basil, dressing, and salt and pepper and mix lightly. Soften the remaining envelope gelatin in the cold water and dissolve over hot water. Cool to lukewarm and mix with the mayonnaise. Combine the vegetables and lobster with the mayonnaise mixture and mix gently but thoroughly. Taste and adjust the seasoning. Turn into the prepared mold. Cover with foil and chill thoroughly until firm.

To serve, unmold on a platter. Garnish with the watercress.

HAM MOUSSE

Remember this savory creation when you have leftover ham.

Serves 4 to 6

1 envelope (1 tablespoon) unflavored
    gelatin
1 cup cold water
1 cup sour cream
1/2 cup Mayonnaise, page 146
2 tablespoons freshly squeezed and
    strained lemon juice
1/4 teaspoon salt
1-1/2 cups ground cooked ham
3/4 teaspoon crushed dried tarragon
    (optional)
3/4 cup finely chopped celery
2 tablespoons finely chopped scallions,
    including 2 inches of the green tops
Leaf lettuce leaves
Pimiento-stuffed olives, sliced

In a saucepan soften the the gelatin in the water. Stir over low heat until the gelatin dissolves. Remove from the heat and cool slightly. Add the sour cream, mayonnaise, lemon juice, and salt and beat until well blended and smooth. Cover and chill until partially set, then whip until fluffy. Fold in the ham, tarragon, celery, and scallions. Taste and adjust the seasoning. Pour into a rinsed and chilled 5-1/2-cup mold. Cover with foil and chill thoroughly until firm.

To serve, unmold on a platter lined with the lettuce and garnish with the olives.

Note You may use a ring mold for the ham mousse and fill the center with potato salad just before serving.

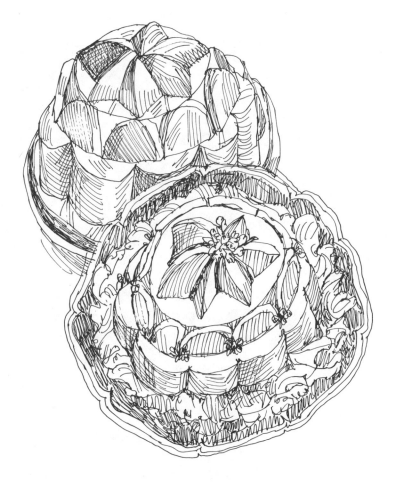

CURRIED CHICKEN MOLD

Serves 4

1 envelope (1 tablespoon) unflavored
  gelatin
3/4 cup cold water
6 ounces rich chicken broth
1/2 cup Mayonnaise, page 146
1 tablespoon freshly squeezed and
  strained lemon juice
1 tablespoon finely chopped scallions,
  including 2 inches of the green tops
1 teaspoon curry powder
1 cup diced cooked chicken
1/2 cup finely diced celery
Lettuce leaves
2 small tomatoes, sliced
2 hard-cooked eggs, sliced
Pitted black olives

In a saucepan soften the gelatin in the
water. Stir over low heat until the gelatin is dissolved. Remove from the heat.
Add the chicken broth, mayonnaise,
lemon juice, scallions, and curry powder and beat until well blended and
smooth. Cover and chill until partially
set. Fold in the chicken and celery.
Taste and adjust the seasoning. Pour
into a rinsed and chilled 1-quart mold.
Cover with foil and chill thoroughly
until firm.

  To serve, unmold on a platter lined
with the lettuce leaves and garnish
with the tomatoes, eggs, and olives.

GINGER ALE SALAD

Serves 6 to 8

1 envelope (1 tablespoon) unflavored
  gelatin
1/2 cup cold water
1/4 cup sugar
1-1/2 cups ginger ale
2 tablespoons freshly squeezed and
  strained lemon juice
1 small orange, peeled, seeded, and
  sectioned (remove the white
  membrane)
2 medium peaches, peeled, pitted, and
  sliced
1/2 cup strawberries, hulled and sliced
1/2 cup halved seeded grapes
1 tablespoon very finely chopped
  crystallized ginger (optional)
Sour Cream and Strawberry Dressing,
  page 158

In a small saucepan soften the gelatin
in the water. Stir over low heat until
the gelatin dissolves. Add the sugar
and stir until it dissolves. Remove
from the heat and pour the mixture
into a deep bowl. Stir in the ginger ale
and lemon juice. Chill until the jelly is
thick and syrupy. Stir in the orange,
peaches, strawberries, grapes, and
crystallized ginger. Pour into a rinsed
and chilled 1-quart mold. Cover with
foil and chill thoroughly until firm.
Unmold on a plate and serve with the
sour cream and strawberry dressing.

SWEDISH FROZEN FRUIT SALAD

Serves 4

1 3-ounce package cream cheese, at
  room temperature
1 cup heavy cream, chilled
2 tablespoons freshly squeezed and
  strained lemon juice
2 tablespoons sugar
1/8 teaspoon salt
2 cups cut-up fruit, such as peaches,
  pears, cherries, and green grapes,
  sweetened to taste (peel, core,
  and seed the fruit as necessary
  before cutting)
Leaf lettuce leaves (optional)

Beat the cream cheese with 2 tablespoons of the cream, lemon juice,
sugar, and salt. Whip the remaining
cream and fold into the cheese mixture. Gently stir in the fruit. Turn into
a refrigerator tray. Cover with foil and
freeze until almost firm. Cut the salad
in slices and serve on the lettuce
leaves, if desired.

WINE JELLY WITH FRUIT

Serves 4

1 envelope (1 tablespoon) unflavored
    gelatin
1/2 cup cold water
1-1/2 cups rosé or port wine
1/2 cup sugar
Rind of 1/2 lemon
1/4 cup halved pitted cherries or
    strawberries
3/4 cup sliced peaches
3/4 cup sliced banana
1/2 cup heavy cream, whipped, sweet-
    ened, and flavored with vanilla
    extract

Soak the gelatin in the water. In an enameled saucepan bring the wine, 1/4 cup of the sugar, and the lemon rind to a boil over moderate heat, stirring constantly to dissolve the sugar. Reduce the heat to low and simmer 5 minutes. Add the gelatin and stir until it dissolves. Remove from the heat and discard the lemon rind.

Pour a 1/2-inch layer of the liquid gelatin into a rinsed and chilled 1-quart mold. Chill until set. Arrange the cherries cut side up on the set gelatin. Sprinkle with some of the remaining sugar. Pour in 1/2 inch more of the liquid gelatin. Chill again until set. Continue with layers of fruit, sugar, and liquid gelatin, ending with liquid gelatin. (Heat the liquid gelatin slightly if it sets before being used.) Cover the mold with foil and chill thoroughly until firm. Unmold on a plate and serve as a dessert with the flavored whipped cream.

CRANBERRY-WINE MOLD

Serves 4

1 envelope (1 tablespoon) unflavored
    gelatin
1/4 cup cold water
3/4 cup rosé or port wine
1-1/4 cups sugar
1/4 cup cranberry juice
1 tablespoon freshly squeezed and
    strained lemon juice
2 cups cranberries, picked over and
    washed

Soak the gelatin in the water. In an enameled saucepan bring the wine, 6 tablespoons of the sugar, cranberry juice, and lemon juice to a boil over moderate heat, stirring constantly to dissolve the sugar. Remove from the heat, add the gelatin, and stir until it dissolves. Place the pan over a bowl of ice and let the mixture cool, stirring from time to time, until it thickens. Do not allow it to set. Pour the jelly mixture into a rinsed and chilled 1-quart mold. Cover with foil and refrigerate until it is well set.

In a saucepan combine the cranberries with enough water barely to cover them. Bring to a boil over moderate heat and cook 20 minutes. Remove from the heat and force the berries and the liquid through a fine sieve into a saucepan. Stir in the remaining sugar and simmer the purée 3 minutes. Remove from the heat and cool 15 minutes. Fill the mold with the cranberry purée. Cover and chill overnight. Unmold on a plate and serve as an accompaniment to roast turkey.

Salad Dressings

The success of any salad is ultimately determined by the excellence of its dressing. Although the majority of salads require a piquant dressing, some are greatly enhanced by a sweet one. I have suggested suitable dressings for the individual salads in this book. Familiarize yourself with the different types of dressings and the salads they best complement. For instance, a light, tart, French-type dressing is ideal for green salads since it allows one to enjoy their color as well as texture. A heavy dressing will cause any lettuce except iceberg to collapse.

Although an extremely wide choice of bottled dressings is available in markets, homemade dressings are superior in taste and more economical than commercial preparations. For a discussion of salad dressing ingredients please consult pages 15 to 27.

In this chapter you will find, along with classic mayonnaise and French-type salad dressings, a number of exotic and little-known recipes that can turn even an ordinary salad into a memorable one. Also included are several recipes for low-calorie dressings that can be enjoyed by weight watchers with a clear conscience.

Although most salad dressings will keep under refrigeration for a day or two, they taste best when freshly made.

Salad Dressings

FRENCH DRESSING
(Vinaigrette)

Although I am fond of French dressing, I have an aversion to what too often passes for it in this country—a heavy, greasy reddish mess that bears no relation whatever to, and must be carefully distinguished from, the authentic vinaigrette dressing of France outlined below.

Makes about 1/2 cup
2 tablespoons wine vinegar
1/4 teaspoon salt
Freshly ground black pepper to taste
6 to 8 tablespoons olive oil

Place all the ingredients in a covered jar and shake vigorously until blended. Or combine the vinegar, salt, and pepper in a small bowl. Stir well to dissolve the salt, then gradually beat in the oil.

Note One-fourth teaspoon dry mustard or Dijon-style mustard may be added with the salt. One tablespoon each wine vinegar and fresh lemon juice are sometimes substituted for the vinegar.

FRENCH DRESSING VARIATIONS

Garlic French Dressing To French Dressing add 1 small clove garlic, crushed.

Onion French Dressing To French Dressing add 1 tablespoon minced shallots or scallions.

Herb French Dressing To French Dressing add finely chopped fresh or crushed dried herbs such as parsley, basil, dill, tarragon, oregano, and chives, alone or in combination. The choice of herb (or herbs) depends on the particular salad. Consult page 24 for suggestions.

Egg and Olive French Dressing To French Dressing add 1 hard-cooked egg, chopped, and 4 pimiento-stuffed olives, chopped. Very good for a salad of mixed greens.

Avocado French Dressing Peel and mash 1/2 avocado. Gradually beat in French Dressing and continue to beat until smooth. Serve at once on sliced tomatoes or citrus fruits.

Sesame Seed French Dressing To French Dressing add 1/4 cup toasted sesame seeds and 1 small clove garlic, crushed (optional). Delightful on cooked vegetables such as beets or cauliflower. (To toast sesame seeds: Spread on a baking sheet in a preheated 350° oven about 15 minutes or until golden brown. Stir occasionally, watching closely to prevent burning.)

LEMON FRENCH DRESSING

Makes about 1/2 cup
3 tablespoons or more freshly
   squeezed and strained lemon juice
1/4 teaspoon salt
Freshly ground black pepper to taste
6 tablespoons olive oil

Place all the ingredients in a covered jar and shake vigorously until blended. Or combine the lemon juice, salt, and pepper in a small bowl. Stir well to dissolve the salt, then gradually beat in the oil. More lemon juice may be added, if desired.

Note One-fourth teaspoon dry mustard and 1 small clove garlic, crushed, are sometimes added to this dressing.

Curry-Lemon French Dressing Variation Add 1/4 teaspoon curry powder, 1 tablespoon minced scallions, and, if you like, 1 tablespoon minced peeled and seeded tomato. Excellent with seafood, chicken, meats, or vegetables.

LIME FRENCH DRESSING

Makes about 3/4 cup
1/2 cup olive oil
3 tablespoons freshly squeezed and
    strained lime juice
1/2 teaspoon grated lime rind
1 tablespoon grated mild onion
    (optional)
Salt and freshly ground black pepper
    to taste

Combine all the ingredients in a small
bowl and beat with a fork or whisk
until well blended.

FRUIT FRENCH DRESSING

This complements tart apples and citrus fruits.

Makes about 1/2 cup
2 tablespoons freshly squeezed and
    strained grapefruit juice
1 tablespoon freshly squeezed and
    strained lemon juice
1/8 teaspoon salt
Dash paprika
1/4 teaspoon superfine sugar
    (optional)
1/4 cup olive oil

Place all the ingredients in a covered
jar and shake vigorously until blended.

Salad Dressings

HEAVY CREAM FRENCH DRESSING

This can grace a bowlful of mixed greens.

Makes about 1/2 cup
1/4 cup olive oil
2 tablespoons red wine vinegar
2 tablespoons heavy cream
1 small clove garlic, crushed
1 tablespoon lightly toasted sesame
    seeds, page 138
1/2 teaspoon salt
Freshly ground black pepper to taste

Put all the ingredients in a covered jar and shake vigorously until blended.

CURRY FRUIT FRENCH DRESSING

Marvelous with citrus fruits.

Makes 3/4 cup
1 teaspoon superfine sugar
1/2 teaspoon salt
1/8 teaspoon dry mustard
1/4 teaspoon curry powder or to taste
1/4 cup freshly squeezed and strained
    lemon juice
1/4 cup freshly squeezed and strained
    grapefruit juice
1/3 cup olive oil

Combine the sugar, salt, mustard, and curry powder in a small bowl. Add the lemon juice and grapefruit juice and mix well. Gradually beat in the oil until well blended.

MEXICAN DRESSING

Makes 1/2 cup
1/4 cup olive oil
1-1/2 tablespoons freshly squeezed and
    strained lemon juice
1-1/2 tablespoons freshly squeezed and
    strained orange juice
1 tablespoon unsweetened pineapple
    juice
1/2 to 1 teaspoon superfine sugar
1/4 teaspoon salt
1/8 teaspoon dry mustard
Dash chili powder

Combine all the ingredients in a small bowl and beat until well blended. Very good with apples, avocados, bananas, oranges, grapefruit, or pineapple.

ITALIAN DRESSING

Makes about 1/2 cup
1 small clove garlic
1 teaspoon salt
2 tablespoons wine vinegar
1-1/2 tablespoons freshly squeezed
    and strained lemon juice
6 tablespoons olive oil
1/2 teaspoon freshly ground black
    pepper

In a small bowl mash the garlic with
the salt. Add the vinegar and lemon
juice and stir well. Add the oil and
pepper and beat with a fork or whisk
until thoroughly blended. Remove and
discard any remaining bits of garlic.
Beat again just before serving.

Note Various seasonings such as basil,
oregano, dry mustard, minced scallions, tomato, and anchovies, used
according to taste, are sometimes
added to this dressing. The lemon juice
may be omitted.

CATALAN DRESSING

Lively and highly seasoned—a classic
dressing for chicory.

Makes 3/4 cup
1/2 cup olive oil
1/4 cup wine vinegar
2 to 3 cloves garlic, crushed
8 toasted blanched almonds, ground
1 fresh red chili pepper, seeded and
    ground, or cayenne pepper to taste
3/4 teaspoon salt or to taste

Combine all the ingredients in a small
bowl. Beat with a fork or whisk until
thoroughly blended.

ANCHOVY AND BEET DRESSING

Makes about 1 cup
2 tablespoons wine vinegar
6 tablespoons olive oil
1 small clove garlic, crushed
1 slice onion, finely chopped
1/2 teaspoon salt
1/8 teaspoon freshly ground black
    pepper
3 anchovy fillets, chopped
3 tablespoons peeled and diced cooked
    beets
1 hard-cooked egg, chopped

Place all the ingredients in a covered
jar and shake thoroughly.

CHIFFONADE DRESSING

Serve this for a change on mixed
greens.

Makes 1-1/2 cups
1 tablespoon wine vinegar
1 tablespoon freshly squeezed and
    strained lemon juice
1/4 teaspoon salt
1/4 teaspoon dry mustard
6 tablespoons olive oil
Freshly ground black pepper to taste
1 tablespoon finely chopped scallions
    or onion
2 tablespoons finely chopped parsley
1 to 2 hard-cooked eggs, chopped
2 tablespoons well drained, peeled,
    and julienne-cut cooked beets

Place all the ingredients in a covered
jar and shake thoroughly.

ANCHOVY-CHEESE DRESSING

Makes about 1 cup
1/2 cup olive oil
2 tablespoons wine vinegar
1 tablespoon freshly squeezed and
    strained lemon juice
1 2-ounce can anchovy fillets
1-1/2 ounces cream cheese, at room
    temperature
1/4 cup chopped mild white onion
1 tiny clove garlic, crushed, or
    1/4 teaspoon garlic salt
Dash Tabasco sauce
1/2 tablespoon water

Combine all the ingredients in the container of an electric blender. Cover and whirl until well blended and smooth. If you do not have a blender, mash the cream cheese with a fork. Add the anchovy fillets and continue to mash the mixture, gradually adding the oil, then the vinegar and lemon juice until well blended and smooth. Finely mince the onion and add to the cheese and anchovy mixture along with the garlic, Tabasco sauce, and water. Mix until thoroughly blended. Serve with tossed green salads.

AVOCADO DRESSING

Delicious over sliced tomatoes or citrus fruit.

Makes about 1 cup
1 avocado
1/4 cup olive oil
3 tablespoons freshly squeezed and
    strained lemon juice
1/2 teaspoon salt
1/4 teaspoon freshly ground black
    pepper
1/8 teaspoon garlic powder, or
    1 tiny clove garlic, crushed
1/8 teaspoon onion powder, or
    1 slice onion, finely chopped
Dash chili powder
Dash cayenne pepper or Tabasco sauce

Peel, pit, and mash the avocado. Combine the remaining ingredients. Gradually add to the mashed avocado, beating until smooth. Serve immediately.

AVOCADO CREAM DRESSING

Makes about 1-1/2 cups
2 tablespoons freshly squeezed and
    strained lemon or lime juice
1/2 cup heavy cream
1 avocado, peeled, pitted, and diced
3 tablespoons confectioners' sugar or
    to taste
1/8 teaspoon ground ginger
1/8 teaspoon salt
1/4 cup heavy cream, whipped
    (optional)

Place all the ingredients except the whipped cream in the container of an electric blender. Cover and whirl until well blended and smooth. If you do not have a blender, mash the avocado with a fork, gradually adding the lemon juice and heavy cream until well blended and smooth. Add the confectioners' sugar, ginger, and salt and mix thoroughly. Fold in the whipped cream until thoroughly combined. Serve with fruit salads.

Salad Dressings

MAYONNAISE

This famous dressing, which has been made by hand for more than three centuries, can also be prepared very successfully and virtually effortlessly with an electric mixer or in an electric blender. Commercial mayonnaise has little resemblance to the homemade product, which takes so little time and tastes so good that once you have made your own it is difficult to settle for the store-bought variety.

Mayonnaise made by hand is easiest to prepare when all ingredients are at room temperature. The choice of oil is a matter of taste. I prefer using 1/2 vegetable oil and 1/2 olive oil since I find the former too bland when used alone and the latter too strong when used in large amounts.

Don't attempt to make mayonnaise if a thunderstorm is on its way or is in progress for it will not bind. To prevent dangerous spoilage, take care to store mayonnaise in a tightly closed container in the refrigerator, where it will keep up to 5 days.

Makes about 1 cup
1 large egg yolk
1/2 teaspoon salt
1/2 teaspoon dry mustard
2 tablespoons freshly squeezed and
   strained lemon juice or white
   wine vinegar
1 cup vegetable oil, olive oil, or a
   combination of each

In a mixing bowl beat the egg yolk with a large wire whisk or an electric mixer about 1 minute or so. Add the salt and mustard and beat another minute. Add the lemon juice and beat vigorously. Start adding the oil, a few drops at a time, while beating continuously, until about 1/2 cup of the oil has been used and the mixture has thickened. Beat in the remaining oil, adding it about 1 tablespoon at a time. If the mayonnaise becomes too thick, thin it with drops of lemon juice. Use the mayonnaise immediately, or transfer it to a small bowl or jar, cover, and refrigerate for future use.

Note One-fourth teaspoon paprika and/or a dash cayenne pepper may be added with the salt and mustard.

BLENDER MAYONNAISE

This uses the whole egg rather than the yolk alone and is lighter and fluffier than handmade mayonnaise. And it couldn't be easier!

Makes about 1-1/4 cups
1 egg
3/4 teaspoon salt
1/2 teaspoon dry mustard
2 tablespoons freshly squeezed and
   strained lemon juice or
   white wine vinegar, or
   1 tablespoon each lemon juice and
   wine vinegar
1 cup vegetable oil, olive oil, or a
   combination of each

Combine the egg, salt, mustard, lemon juice, and 1/4 cup of the oil in the container of an electric blender. Cover and whirl at high speed until the ingredients are blended. Immediately remove the lid and slowly pour in the remaining 3/4 cup oil in a steady stream until the mixture has thickened. Use the mayonnaise at once, or transfer to a small bowl or jar, cover, and refrigerate for future use.

MAYONNAISE VARIATIONS

Herb Mayonnaise To Mayonnaise add finely chopped fresh or crushed dried herbs such as parsley, basil, tarragon, dill, oregano, and chives, alone or in combination. The choice of herb (or herbs) depends on the particular salad. Consult page 24 for suggestions.

One good combination consists of 2 tablespoons minced parsley, 1 tablespoon minced chives, and 1/4 teaspoon each crushed dried basil and tarragon. Another one, especially good for fish salads, is 2 tablespoons minced parsley, 1 tablespoon minced chives, and 1 teaspoon each minced tarragon and dill. The herbs may be blanched before using.

Green Mayonnaise To Mayonnaise add 8 spinach leaves, chopped. If you like, you may also add 8 sprigs watercress or 1 tablespoon chopped chives or scallion, 1 tablespoon chopped tarragon, and 1 teaspoon each chopped parsley and dill. (The greens may be blanched before using.) Whirl in a blender until smooth and evenly colored. Excellent for salmon, tuna, or other fish salads.

Parsley, Caper, and Olive Mayonnaise To Mayonnaise add 1 cup minced parsley, 2 teaspoons capers, drained and chopped, 8 pimiento-stuffed olives, minced, and 1 small clove garlic, minced. Mix thoroughly. Serve on egg or seafood salads.

Curry Mayonnaise To Mayonnaise add 1 teaspoon curry powder, 1 tiny clove garlic, crushed (optional), and 1 teaspoon freshly squeezed and strained lemon or lime juice. Mix well. An excellent dressing for egg, artichoke, potato, rice, meat, or seafood salads.

Garlic Mayonnaise To Mayonnaise add 1 to 2 cloves garlic, crushed. Mix until thoroughly smooth. Serve with seafood or vegetable salads.

Egg Mayonnaise To Mayonnaise add 1 hard-cooked egg, minced, and 1 teaspoon minced onion. Mix until smooth. In another variation the mayonnaise is combined with 2 hard-cooked eggs, minced, 1 teaspoon prepared mustard, 1 tablespoon fresh lemon juice, and 1/8 teaspoon Tabasco sauce. Especially good on lobster, crab, avocado, or tomato salads.

Tuna Mayonnaise To Mayonnaise add 1 7-ounce can tuna, drained and flaked, 1 small clove garlic, crushed, 1/2 teaspoon crushed dried oregano or basil, and 1 teaspoon anchovy paste or to taste. Whirl in a blender until smooth. Serve with sliced tomatoes, hard-cooked eggs, or cooked green beans.

Caviar Mayonnaise To Mayonnaise add 1/3 cup imported black or red caviar, 1 tablespoon minced onion or scallion, 2 hard-cooked eggs, minced, 1 pimiento, drained and minced, and 2 teaspoons freshly squeezed and strained lemon juice. Mix well. Serve over Belgian endive, Bibb lettuce, or seafood salads.

Shrimp Mayonnaise To Mayonnaise add 1/2 cup sour cream, 1 cup cooked, shelled, and deveined shrimp, ground, 3 hard-cooked egg yolks, sieved, 2 tablespoons grated onion, 2 tablespoons catsup, 1 tablespoon minced parsley, 2 tablespoons light cream, 1 tablespoon freshly squeezed and strained lime juice, 1/2 teaspoon garlic salt, 1/4 teaspoon dry mustard, 1/2 teaspoon paprika, and Tabasco sauce and salt to taste. Blend thoroughly. Serve over crisp wedges of lettuce, sliced tomatoes, or sliced avocados.

Avocado-Shrimp Mayonnaise To Mayonnaise add 1 small avocado, peeled, pitted, and diced, 3 ounces cooked shrimp, diced, 1 scallion, sliced, 2 tablespoons freshly squeezed and strained lemon juice, and salt to taste. Blend until smooth. Delicious on cooked cauliflower, page 62.

Lobster Mayonnaise To Mayonnaise add 1 cup minced cooked lobster meat, 2 tablespoons lobster paste (optional), 1/4 teaspoon dry mustard, and salt to taste. Mix thoroughly. Good with avocado or shrimp molds.

149

Salad Dressings

GREEN GODDESS DRESSING

A famous dressing for seafood or greens, this may also be served as a dip.

Makes about 1-1/2 cups
1 cup Mayonnaise, page 146
1/2 cup sour cream or heavy cream
2 to 3 teaspoons anchovy paste, or
    2 or 3 anchovy fillets, finely
    chopped
2 tablespoons finely chopped chives
    or scallions
1/4 cup finely chopped parsley
1 teaspoon crushed dried tarragon
1 small clove garlic, finely chopped
    (optional)
1 tablespoon freshly squeezed and
    strained lemon juice
1 tablespoon white wine vinegar or
    tarragon vinegar
Salt and freshly ground black pepper
    to taste

Put all the ingredients in the container of an electric blender. Cover and blend until smooth. If you do not have a blender, combine all the ingredients in a small bowl and mix thoroughly. Taste and adjust the seasoning.

RUSSIAN DRESSING

This popular dressing exists in numerous versions. Some people insist that a true Russian dressing must include caviar.

Makes about 1-1/3 cups
1 cup Mayonnaise, page 146
3 tablespoons catsup or chili sauce
1 tablespoon grated onion
1 to 2 tablespoons imported caviar
1 to 2 teaspoons grated horseradish
    (optional)

In a small bowl combine all the ingredients and mix well. Serve on green, vegetable, egg, or shellfish salads.

Russian Dressing Variation I Combine 1 cup mayonnaise with 3 tablespoons catsup or chili sauce, 2 tablespoons minced green pepper or pimiento, 2 tablespoons minced chives or scallions, and 1 tablespoon freshly squeezed and strained lemon juice. One-half hard-cooked egg, minced, may also be added. Mix well and serve as above.

Russian Dressing Variation II Combine 1/2 cup mayonnaise, 1/2 cup sour cream, 3 tablespoons chili sauce, 3 tablespoons freshly squeezed and strained lime juice, 2 tablespoons minced chives or scallions, and 1/4 teaspoon salt. Mix thoroughly. Try this on avocado or papaya halves filled with crab meat.

THOUSAND ISLAND DRESSING

A favorite creamy, pink dressing for wedges of iceberg lettuce or hard-cooked eggs.

Makes about 1-1/2 cups
1 cup Mayonnaise, page 146
3 tablespoons chili sauce or catsup
1 hard-cooked egg, finely chopped
2 tablespoons finely chopped
    pimiento-stuffed olives
1 tablespoon finely chopped green
    pepper
1 tablespoon finely chopped chives or
    scallions
2 teaspoons finely chopped parsley
1/4 teaspoon paprika (optional)

In a small bowl combine all the ingredients and mix well.

LOUIS DRESSING

This is the dressing used for Crab Louis, a well-known West Coast specialty featuring the highly prized Dungeness crab arranged over a bed of shredded lettuce and garnished with lettuce leaves, wedges of tomato and eggs, black olives, and, sometimes, sliced avocado. Louis dressing is also good with shrimp.

Makes 2 cups
1 cup Mayonnaise, page 146
1/4 cup heavy cream
1/4 cup chili sauce
1/4 cup chopped green pepper
1/4 cup chopped scallions, including
    2 inches of the green tops
2 tablespoons freshly squeezed and
    strained lemon juice
Salt to taste

In a small bowl combine all the ingredients and mix well.

AVOCADO MAYONNAISE

Makes about 1 cup
1/3 cup Mayonnaise, page 146
1 medium avocado, peeled, pitted, and
    diced
1 to 2 tablespoons freshly squeezed
    and strained lemon juice
1/2 teaspoon chili powder
1/8 teaspoon garlic powder
Dash cayenne pepper
1/2 teaspoon salt or to taste

Put all the ingredients in the container of an electric blender. Cover and whirl until well blended and smooth. If you do not have a blender, mash the avocado with a fork, gradually adding the lemon juice and mayonnaise until the mixture is well blended and smooth. Add the remaining ingredients and mix thoroughly. Exceptionally good on sliced tomatoes, vegetable salads, or cold shellfish.

Variation Put 3/4 cup mayonnaise, 1 avocado, peeled, pitted, and diced, 2 scallions, sliced, 2 tablespoons freshly squeezed and strained lemon juice, 1/4 teaspoon garlic powder, and salt to taste in a blender container. Blend and serve as above. Alternately, mash the avocado with a fork, gradually adding the lemon juice and mayonnaise until the mixture is well blended and smooth. Mince the scallions and add to the avocado mixture with the remaining ingredients; mix thoroughly.

Salad Dressings

HONEY-LIME DRESSING I

Makes about 1-1/4 cups
1/2 cup Mayonnaise, page 146
1/4 cup honey
2 tablespoons freshly squeezed and
    strained lime or lemon juice
1/8 teaspoon grated lime or lemon
    rind (optional)
1/2 cup heavy cream, whipped

In a small bowl thoroughly mix together the mayonnaise, honey, lime juice, and lime rind. Fold in the whipped cream until well combined. Good on fruit salads.

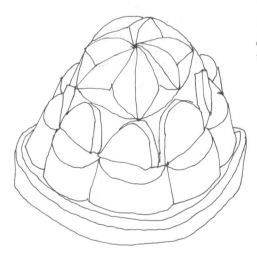

HONEY-LIME DRESSING II

Makes 1/2 cup
1/4 cup honey
1/4 cup freshly squeezed and strained
    lime juice
Grated rind of 1 lime

Combine the ingredients in a small bowl and mix until well blended. A lovely dressing for Persian, Crenshaw, or other cubed melon, alone or mixed with julienne strips of ham or prosciutto. (If desired, you may marinate the melon in port wine in the refrigerator until chilled before mixing it with the dressing and ham, if used.)

Variation Substitute 1/4 teaspoon each ground coriander and nutmeg for the grated lime rind.

BOILED DRESSING

A basic cooked dressing for cole slaw, vegetable, and fruit salads.

Makes 1-1/2 cups
2 tablespoons all-purpose flour
1-1/2 tablespoons sugar
1 teaspoon salt
1 teaspoon dry mustard
Dash cayenne pepper
1 cup milk
2 egg yolks
1/3 cup freshly squeezed and strained
    lemon juice or mild vinegar
2 tablespoons butter

In a small, heavy saucepan combine the flour, sugar, salt, mustard, and cayenne pepper. Gradually stir in the milk. Cook over low heat, stirring con-

stantly, until the mixture comes to a boil. Boil 1 minute. Remove from the heat and set aside.

In a small bowl beat the egg yolks until frothy. Gradually beat in the lemon juice, then stir in the hot mixture from the saucepan, a little at a time. Pour back into the saucepan. Cook over low heat, stirring constantly, until the mixture comes to a boil. Boil 1 minute. Remove from the heat and stir in the butter. Cool. Refrigerate, covered, until ready to use.

Note Celery or dill seeds or chopped parsley, chives, or other herbs are sometimes added to this dressing.

Sour Cream Variation To 1/2 cup chilled Boiled Dressing, fold in 1 cup sour cream. Use for vegetable salads.

Whipped Cream Variation To 1/2 cup chilled Boiled Dressing, fold in 1/2 cup heavy cream, whipped. Use for fruit salads.

Salad Dressings

TARATOOR BI TAHINI
(Sesame Sauce)

If your travels have led you to the Middle East, you are no doubt familiar with this versatile sauce, which makes an excellent dressing for avocado slices, boiled cauliflower, hard-cooked eggs, or seafood. It may also be served as an appetizer or dip, accompanied by Arab or French bread.

Makes about 1-1/2 cups
1 to 2 large cloves garlic
Salt
1 cup *tahini* (see page 73)
Cold water as needed
Juice of 3 lemons or to taste, freshly
    squeezed and strained
1/4 cup finely chopped parsley

In a deep bowl crush the garlic with a pinch of the salt. Add the *tahini* and mix well. Gradually beat in 1/4 cup water, the lemon juice, and an additional 1/2 teaspoon salt. Continue beating vigorously, adding more water as needed, a spoonful or so at a time, until the mixture attains a thick, creamy texture. Taste and adjust the seasoning, adding more salt and lemon juice to taste.

This mixture, which can be quickly and easily prepared in an electric blender, is served as is or garnished with chopped parsley. It is also delicious seasoned with ground cumin or curry powder or sprinkled with toasted sesame seeds.

SESAME SAUCE WITH AVOCADO

A more sophisticated cousin of the preceding recipe, this goes well with boiled cauliflower, seafood, or sliced tomatoes, or as a dip with potato or tortilla chips.

Makes about 1 cup
1 medium ripe avocado
1/4 cup Taratoor bi Tahini, preceding

Peel, pit, and mash the avocado until smooth, or whirl in an electric blender. Add the taratoor bi tahini and blend well. Taste and adjust the seasoning.

SATSIVI
(Walnut Sauce)

This distinctive sauce, which comes from the Soviet republic of Georgia in the Caucasus, enhances a combination of cucumbers, tomatoes, and celery as well as cooked green beans, red beans, asparagus, spinach, and beets. It has fewer calories than most dressings.

Makes about 3/4 cup
1/2 cup walnut halves (preferably
    freshly shelled)
1 small clove garlic
1/4 teaspoon salt or to taste
2 tablespoons wine vinegar
1/4 cup water
2 tablespoons finely chopped onion
    (optional)
2 tablespoons finely chopped
    coriander, or
    1/2 teaspoon ground coriander
Cayenne pepper to taste

Pound the walnuts to a paste with the garlic and salt. Stir in the vinegar and water and blend well. Add the onion, coriander, and cayenne and mix thoroughly. If the mixture seems too thick, a little more water may be added. Taste and adjust the seasoning.

SKORDALIA
(Garlic Sauce)

A famous Greek specialty traditionally served with seafood or cooked vegetables such as sliced beets.

Makes about 1 cup
3 to 4 cloves garlic, finely chopped
Salt
2 medium potatoes, cooked, peeled, and mashed while still warm
About 1/2 cup olive oil
2 tablespoons freshly squeezed and strained lemon juice or to taste
Freshly ground black pepper to taste

With a large mortar and pestle crush the garlic and 1 teaspoon salt to a fine paste. Add the potatoes, a little at a time, stirring and mashing vigorously. Beat in the oil, a spoonful or so at a time, then the lemon juice and salt and pepper to taste. Taste and adjust the seasoning, adding more oil or lemon juice if needed. For a thinner sauce, beat in lukewarm water 1/4 teaspoon at a time until of desired consistency.

Note One egg yolk may be beaten into the mashed potato and garlic mixture before beating in the oil. White wine vinegar may be used instead of the lemon juice. There also exist versions of *skordalia* that substitute crustless slices of white bread, soaked in water and squeezed dry, for the potatoes. Ground blanched almonds or walnuts are sometimes pounded with the garlic and salt before adding the bread or potatoes.

TOMATO DRESSING

A good dressing for weight watchers.

Makes about 2/3 cup
1/2 cup tomato juice
1 hard-cooked egg yolk, mashed
1-1/2 tablespoons freshly squeezed and strained lemon juice, or
   1 tablespoon red wine vinegar
1 scallion, finely chopped, including 2 inches of the green tops
1 teaspoon finely chopped basil or dill
Garlic powder to taste
Salt and freshly ground black pepper to taste

Combine all the ingredients in a small bowl and mix until thoroughly blended. (The egg white may be minced and sprinkled over the salad.)

Salad Dressings

GARLIC YOGURT DRESSING I

High in flavor but low in calories, this is a tasty dressing for cooked asparagus, beets, green beans, or spinach.

Makes 1 cup
1 medium clove garlic or to taste
1/4 teaspoon salt
1 cup unflavored yogurt

In a small bowl, crush the garlic with the salt to a smooth paste. Add the yogurt and beat until thoroughly blended.

Note One tablespoon minced mint (or 1/2 teaspoon crushed dried mint) and/or dill may be added. Or instead of the garlic you may season the yogurt with minced scallions or chives, lemon juice, and curry powder.

GARLIC YOGURT DRESSING II

Makes about 1-1/4 cups
1 medium clove garlic
1/2 teaspoon salt or to taste
1 cup unflavored yogurt
Juice of 1 lemon or lime, freshly
    squeezed and strained
2 tablespoons olive oil or to taste

In a small bowl, crush the garlic with the salt to a smooth paste. Add the yogurt. Stir in the lemon juice and oil and beat until thoroughly blended. Taste and adjust the seasoning. Serve over cucumbers, spinach, or lettuce.

Note One-fourth teaspoon crushed dried oregano or 1 teaspoon paprika may be added to the dressing.

SWEET YOGURT DRESSING

Calorie-wise, refreshing, and unusual. Serve over dessert salads or fruit.

Makes 1 cup
1 cup unflavored yogurt
2 tablespoons confectioners'
    sugar or to taste
1/4 teaspoon ground cinnamon, or
    2 or 3 drops vanilla extract

Spoon the yogurt into a small bowl. Beat in the sugar and then the cinnamon until well blended.

Note Yogurt is also good flavored with raspberry syrup or orange flower water, which is available at Middle Eastern groceries and some gourmet shops.

YOGURT AND HONEY DRESSING

A delectable, low-calorie dressing to serve with fruit salads.

Makes about 1 cup
1 cup unflavored yogurt
2 tablespoons honey
1 tablespoon finely chopped mint
2 teaspoons freshly squeezed and
    strained lemon or lime juice

Combine all the ingredients in a bowl and beat together until well blended.

SOUR CREAM AND DILL DRESSING

Makes about 1 cup
1 cup sour cream
1-1/2 tablespoons finely chopped dill
1 teaspoon grated onion
2 teaspoons freshly squeezed and
    strained lemon juice
1/2 teaspoon salt or to taste
Pinch freshly ground white pepper

Combine all the ingredients in a small bowl. Mix well. Taste and adjust the seasoning. Cover and chill thoroughly. Good with Salmon Mousse, page 128.

SOUR CREAM AND VEGETABLE DRESSING

Serve this crunchy and delightful dressing over lettuce or cabbage.

Makes about 1-1/2 cups
1 cup sour cream
1/2 cup finely chopped peeled and
    seeded (if necessary) cucumber
2 tablespoons finely chopped green or
    sweet red pepper
2 tablespoons finely chopped scallions,
    including 2 inches of the green tops
1 tablespoon finely chopped dill or
    basil (optional)
1 teaspoon freshly squeezed and
    strained lemon or lime juice
1/2 teaspoon salt
Dash freshly ground white pepper

Combine all the ingredients in a small bowl. Mix well. Taste and adjust the seasoning. Cover and chill thoroughly.

SOUR CREAM AND SHRIMP DRESSING

Makes about 2 cups
1 cup sour cream
8 ounces cooked shrimp, shelled,
    deveined, and diced
1 tablespoon grated onion
2 to 4 tablespoons catsup
1 tablespoon freshly squeezed and
    strained lemon juice
1 teaspoon grated horseradish
    (optional)
1 tiny clove garlic, crushed, or
    1/4 teaspoon garlic salt
1/4 teaspoon paprika
Pinch dry mustard
Salt to taste

Combine all the ingredients in a small bowl and mix thoroughly. Taste and adjust the seasoning. Cover and chill. A good dressing for a mayonnaise-based avocado mold or sliced tomatoes.

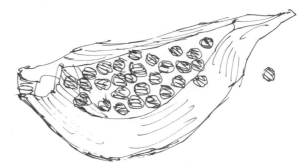

Salad Dressings

SOUR CREAM AND ROQUEFORT DRESSING

This will flatter mixed greens or tomatoes.

Makes about 1-1/3 cups
2 ounces Roquefort cheese,
    crumbled
1 cup sour cream
1 teaspoon finely chopped onion or
    shallots
1/2 teaspoon dry mustard
1/2 teaspoon salt

In a small bowl mash the cheese, gradually adding the sour cream until the mixture is well blended and smooth. Add the onion, mustard, and salt and mix thoroughly.

SOUR CREAM AND STRAWBERRY DRESSING

Heavenly on fruit salads.

Makes about 2 cups
1-1/2 cups sour cream
1-1/4 cups strawberries, hulled,
    sliced and sweetened, or
1 10-ounce package frozen sweetened
    strawberries, thawed

Combine the sour cream and strawberries in a bowl. Stir until well blended. Cover and chill.

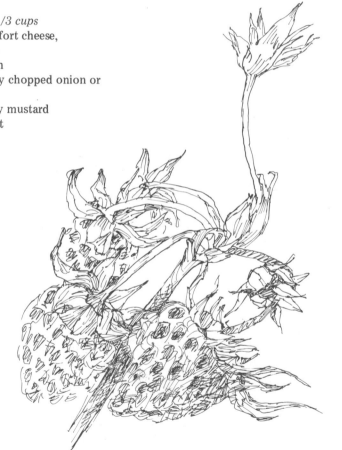

SOUR CREAM AND HONEY DRESSING

Makes about 1 cup
1 cup sour cream
1-1/2 tablespoons honey
1-1/2 teaspoons freshly squeezed and
    strained lemon or lime juice
1/4 teaspoon salt

Combine all the ingredients in a bowl. Stir until well blended. Cover and chill. Good with fruit salads.

CREAM AND HONEY DRESSING

Makes about 1 cup
1/2 cup heavy cream, chilled
3 tablespoons honey
2 teaspoons freshly squeezed and
    strained orange juice
1 teaspoon freshly squeezed and
    strained lemon juice

In a chilled bowl whip the cream with a whisk or a rotary or electric beater until medium thick. Combine the honey, orange juice, and lemon juice. Add to the cream and beat until well blended. Serve with fruit salads.

SOUR CREAM, HONEY, AND CRÈME DE MENTHE DRESSING

Makes about 1-1/2 cups
1 cup sour cream
1 tablespoon honey or to taste
1-1/2 tablespoons green crème de
    menthe liqueur
1 drop green food coloring (optional)

Combine all the ingredients in a bowl. Stir until thoroughly blended. Cover and chill. Serve with fruit salads.

Yogurt, Lime, and Crème de Menthe Dressing Variation Combine 1 cup unflavored yogurt, freshly squeezed and strained juice of 3 limes, 2 tablespoons green crème de menthe liqueur, and 1 mint sprig, minced (optional) in a bowl. Stir until well blended. Chill and serve as above.

SOUR CREAM, HONEY, AND ORANGE RIND DRESSING

Serve over sliced oranges, pears, or other fruit.

Makes about 1 cup
1 cup sour cream
2 tablespoons honey
1/4 teaspoon grated orange rind

Combine all the ingredients in a bowl. Stir until well blended. Cover and chill.

SOUR CREAM, HONEY, AND COCONUT DRESSING

Appropriate for gelatin fruit salads or other fruit salads.

Makes about 1-1/4 cups
1 cup sour cream
2 tablespoons honey
2 teaspoons freshly squeezed and
    strained lemon juice
1/4 cup freshly grated coconut

Combine all the ingredients in a bowl. Stir until well blended. Cover and chill thoroughly.

Salad Dressings

CREAM CHEESE AND CURRANT JELLY DRESSING

Pale pink and elegant.

Makes about 2 cups
1 3-ounce package cream cheese, at
  room temperature
2 tablespoons heavy cream
1 tablespoon freshly squeezed and
  strained lemon juice
Dash salt
1/4 cup currant jelly
3/4 cup heavy cream, whipped

In a chilled bowl mash the cream cheese, gradually stirring in the 2 tablespoons heavy cream and lemon juice until well blended. Add the salt and currant jelly and mix thoroughly. Fold in the whipped cream until well combined. Serve on fruits such as bananas, berries, pears, and cantaloupes.

BANANA CREAM DRESSING

Makes about 2 cups
2 tablespoons brown sugar
2 tablespoons honey
3 medium fully ripe bananas, peeled
  and mashed
1 cup heavy cream, whipped

Combine the brown sugar and honey with the mashed bananas and blend until smooth. Force through a sieve. Fold the whipped cream into the banana mixture. Serve with dessert fruit salads.

APRICOT CREAM DRESSING

Refined and delicate, this makes an exquisite dressing for bananas, pears, or other mild-flavored fruits.

Makes about 1 cup
1 3-ounce package cream cheese,
  at room temperature
1/8 teaspoon salt
2 tablespoons heavy cream
1 teaspoon freshly squeezed and
  strained lemon juice
1/3 cup or more apricot preserves
1 tablespoon apricot liqueur or to taste
1/4 cup heavy cream, whipped

In a chilled bowl mash the cream cheese and salt, gradually stirring in the 2 tablespoons heavy cream and lemon juice until well blended. Add the apricot preserves and apricot liqueur and mix thoroughly. Fold in the whipped cream until smooth.

ORANGE-PINEAPPLE DRESSING

Makes about 1-1/4 cups
2 eggs, slightly beaten
1/4 cup honey
1/4 cup canned pineapple juice
1/2 cup freshly squeezed and
  strained orange juice
1 tablespoon grated orange rind
1/2 cup heavy cream, whipped

Combine all the ingredients except the cream in the top of a double boiler. Cook over hot, not boiling, water about 15 minutes or until thickened, stirring constantly. Remove from the heat, cover, and chill. Fold in the whipped cream until well blended. Serve at once. Fine on dessert salads.

Index

Index

Index

Biographical Data

SONIA UVEZIAN is one of America's most highly acclaimed young cookbook authors. Her first book, *The Cuisine of Armenia* (Harper & Row), was hailed by critics as a triumph and one of the best cookbooks of the year. Equally praised was her next work, *The Best Foods of Russia* (Harcourt Brace Jovanovich). Her recipes have also appeared in *Vogue, Family Circle* and *Prevention* magazines.

Born in Lebanon, Sonia Uvezian received her musical education in Beirut and in New York City. As a concert pianist and with her pianist husband, she has traveled widely and divides her time between the United States and Europe.

WENDY WHEELER is a well-known San Francisco artist who studied art in Florence, Italy, and received her bachelor of fine arts degree *cum laude* from Syracuse University. She is best known for her line drawings, which have been widely published in books, magazines, advertising materials and as a series of greeting cards. But she is also active as a fine artist whose paintings and drawings have been exhibited in museums and art galleries from Florence to San Francisco. She presently works and lives in a studio/home on San Francisco's Telegraph Hill.